CW01024115

RANGE ROVER
SPORT 2005–2013
THE COMPLETE STORY

James Taylor

THE CROWOOD PRESS

First published in 2019 by
The Crowood Press Ltd
Ramsbury, Marlborough
Wiltshire SN8 2HR

enquiries@crowood.com

www.crowood.com

British Library Cataloguing-in-Publication Data
A catalogue record for this book is available from the British Library.

ISBN 978 1 78500 659 3

Typeset and designed by D & N Publishing, Baydon, Wiltshire

Printed and bound in India by Parksons Graphics

CONTENTS

INTRODUCTION AND ACKNOWLEDGEMENTS

As far as I'm aware, this is the first book ever devoted specifically to the first-generation Range Rover Sport. This was a hugely popular model, but it was also controversial: associating the word 'sport' with a Land Rover product immediately raised the hackles of long-standing devotees of the marque, and it took many of them a long time to come to terms with the idea.

It took me a while to get to grips with the Sport, too. When it was released in 2005 I was editor of *Land Rover Enthusiast* magazine, and in a spirit of egalitarianism (which I later regretted) I asked my deputy, Simon Hodder, to go and check out the new model at the press launch in Catalonia. Fortunately, a good relationship with Land Rover themselves enabled me to borrow a TDV6 model for a family holiday in France a year or so later, and I must say that I was impressed. It felt good, not too big like the latest full-size Range Rover, and it went and handled well. Later experience with examples off-road convinced me that this was a proper Land Rover, and a good one.

Of course, its appeal to celebrities gave the Sport a certain image, and a lot of traditional Land Rover folk had difficulties with that. Over the years, though, the Sport has gradually earned itself a place within the Land Rover community. More important from Land Rover's point of view is that this model attracted a whole new set of buyers who had probably never considered buying a Land Rover before, and many of them were convinced enough to stay with the marque. I'm not in any doubt that the first-generation Sport was an enormously important model for Land Rover, and that the company would not be in the largely enviable position it enjoys today without it.

It's customary to include a list of people to thank in the introduction to a book like this. Quite frankly, there are too many to remember, but I am very grateful indeed to the many Land Rover employees who talked to me about the Sport, to the company's press office who provided me with information and photographs when the vehicles were new and who also lent me several examples to try, and to several makers or owners of aftermarket conversions who gave me an insight into what their sectors of the market really appreciated about the model. Lastly, special thanks go to my colleague Jerome André for providing information about the Sport in the USA, which the JLR press office in the USA was unable to source.

James Taylor,
Oxfordshire, April 2019

RANGE ROVER SPORT TIMELINE

2004, January	Preview of the Range Stormer concept at Detroit Motor Show
2005, January	Introduction of the Range Rover Sport at Detroit Motor Show
2005, June	Start of showroom sales: the 2.7-litre TDV6, 4.4-litre V8 and 4.2-litre Supercharged V8 models
2006, November	Introduction of 3.6-litre TDV8 models
2007, September	4.4-litre V8 models withdrawn from Europe but remained available elsewhere
2009, June	Facelifted '2010' models introduced with 3.0-litre TDV6 and 5.0-litre supercharged V8 engines; 3.6-litre TDV8 and 5.0-litre V8 engines available for export
2010, September	4.4-litre TDV8 replaced 3.6-litre, for export only
2011, July	3.0-litre SDV6 engine replaced 3.0-litre TDV6 for most markets
2013, March	Final first-generation Range Rover Sport built

CHAPTER ONE

THE BACKGROUND STORY

To anyone whose first acquaintance with the Land Rover marque was a Range Rover Sport, it probably seems incredible that this high-performance modern SUV (Sport Utility Vehicle) was ultimately derived from a farm runabout. But in order to understand why the Sport became the vehicle it was, it really does help to understand something of the history behind it. A knowledge of that history also helps to explain why many long-term Land Rover devotees turned their noses up at the Sport when it first appeared, for the Sport was the first step in a new direction for Land Rover. It was also a very important turning point for the company, and its success underpinned the new direction that Land Rover would take in the later 2000s – and would take very successfully.

ORIGINS OF THE ROVER COMPANY

Back, though, to that farm runabout, which was the start of the whole Land Rover story in 1948. Back, too, to a British motor manufacturer that no longer exists, but in 1948 was a highly respected independent maker of cars for the professional classes. The Rover Company, like many other car makers, could trace its origins back to the bicycle era of the late nineteenth century; it began to make cars in 1904, and after some difficult times in the 1920s, had returned to prosperity with a strong product line in the 1930s.

Behind Rover's revival were two brothers. The older was Spencer Wilks, whose expertise was in business management, and who became Rover's Managing Director. The younger was Maurice Wilks, a talented engineer who took over the leadership of the engineering teams at Rover. It was the solid reputation that these two – and a similarly talented if rather conservative management team – built for Rover

that persuaded the Air Ministry to ask the company to manage a pair of 'shadow factories' on its behalf in the late 1930s.

The 'shadow factories' came about as the threat of a second war with Germany became more and more real. It was already clear that aircraft would play a major role in any future war, and the Air Ministry wanted to ensure that Britain's ability to produce new warplanes could not be knocked out by enemy bombing. The solution was to disperse aircraft production facilities around the country, by building new factories to 'shadow' those of the established manufacturers. These factories were to be managed by Britain's car makers, who had the experience necessary to oversee large-scale industrial production.

Rover was allocated two factories, one at Acocks Green near Birmingham, and the other at Solihull to the south-east

The former 'shadow' factory at Lode Lane in Solihull became Rover's headquarters in the mid-1940s; this picture dates from shortly after that time.

The main administrative block is readily recognizable in this more recent picture taken at the Solihull plant, but the rest of the site has been extensively redeveloped over the years.

of that city. When war did come in 1939, it proved every bit as devastating as the government had feared. Rover's headquarters and assembly plant in Coventry were rendered unusable during the 'blitz' bombing of that city in 1940, and those staff who had not been called up to fight were dispersed elsewhere. Many of the engineers went north, to assist in the development of Frank Whittle's jet aircraft engine at a series of locations in old textile mills in Lancashire and Yorkshire. Car development stopped altogether.

THE LAND ROVER IS BORN

As the war ended in 1945, Rover's primary job was to return to normality. But it would have to be a new normality. There was no factory or headquarters to return to, and the

company's directors seized upon the government's offer of moving into the former aero-engine factory at Solihull. So it was here that plans for new post-war models were developed, although the task was a difficult one. Even though car production in Europe had been at a standstill for some years, car production in the USA had not been halted until 1942, and when the USA returned to building new models in 1945, those new models had features that were far in advance of anything that Europe could offer.

For Rover, the situation was critical. Out of necessity, the British government was also rationing supplies of raw materials such as steel, and manufacturers were to be allocated supplies on the basis of their export performance. Exports were desperately needed to bring in revenue to rebuild the war-damaged economy, so the scheme's rationale was sound and practical. Rover's problem was that it had no new

HUE 166, with chassis number R.01, was the first pilot-production Land Rover from 1948, and is now a much valued and still quite active museum piece. It was pictured during the seventieth anniversary of Land Rover as a marque, in 2018.

models ready to put into production. All it could do was go into production with warmed-over pre-war designs as a temporary measure – and these were not going to succeed in export markets where they came up against the latest American designs.

So there was a desperate need for a new product that would sell well in export markets, and it was Maurice Wilks who came up with the solution. He had bought a war-surplus Jeep in 1947, and had quickly come to realize how useful it was as a multi-purpose runabout, farm vehicle and even leisure vehicle. The Jeep had created a demand for simple and robust transport wherever it had been seen during the war, and Wilks realized that Rover could build a similar vehicle, using many major components in production for the company's cars. Aimed at agricultural and light industrial users – and it soon became a military vehicle as well – the Land Rover was designed in record time and was in production by summer 1948.

It was an immediate and massive success, far greater than even its manufacturers had imagined might be possible. All thoughts of it being a short-term temporary product were abandoned, and over the next two decades the Land Rover became the primary product of the Rover Company. There were still elegant and well-engineered Rover cars to remind the company of its origins, but the investment that made them possible came largely from the Land Rover.

THE RANGE ROVER IS BORN

The next important step in the company's evolution came in 1970. Spen King, a nephew of the Wilks brothers and an innovative engineer at Rover, realized that it would be possible to create a more comfortable Land Rover designed primarily to carry passengers by using the long-travel suspension that he had drawn up for the company's last new saloon car, the 1963 Rover 2000. Adding all-round disc brakes (again from the 2000), and using the V8 engine that Rover had taken over from General Motors in the USA, would give far better road performance than could be offered by any Land Rover. And so in 1970 the Range Rover was born as a sort of super Land Rover.

Once again, worldwide demand for Rover's new product outstripped supply by a huge margin, and this time the customers discovered in the new product something much more than a comfortable Land Rover. The Range Rover quickly became a prestige purchase, and although in the early days it was no luxury car, many people considered it as a realistic alternative to one. The obvious course of development was held back for many years because in 1968 Rover had been absorbed into British Leyland, and in the 1970s British Leyland had to devote most of its resources to its ailing volume cars division (formerly Austin and Morris), and could not afford to invest in improvements to a model that was already selling more than Rover could make.

Another first: YVB 153H was the first pilot-production Range Rover to leave the Despatch Department at Solihull (which was a holding area for newly assembled vehicles before they were despatched out to a user or dealer). It was the start of a new direction for the Land Rover marque.

This was the third-generation Range Rover, or L322, which became available as a 2002 model and was in production when the Range Rover Sport was launched. It was a highly sophisticated model, and rather larger than the Sport.

A Sporty Range Rover

Land Rover itself chose to develop the Range Rover as a luxury model, for the simple reason that a luxury 4×4 seemed to be what most of its customers wanted. But within the original concept of the Range Rover there had been the

basic concept of a 4×4 with much enhanced road behaviour and exciting performance, and it was those aspects of this multi-sided vehicle that stood out for some buyers.

To meet the expectations of that buyer group, Arthur Silverton established a Range Rover conversions business as an offshoot of the company whose British operations he

Overfinch specialized in adding extra performance and handling to the original Range Rover, successfully exploiting the first stirrings of a market that would develop into the customer base for the Range Rover Sport.

directed. Schuler Presses (who made machine tools) gave birth to Schuler-branded Range Rovers, which from the mid-1970s incorporated a whole range of enhancements. There were higher-performance engines, quieter transmissions that included automatic options (not available on the original Range Rover), braking and suspension enhancements, and a host of other items that really presaged what the Range Rover Sport would achieve thirty years later.

Schuler eventually tired of having their name associated with Range Rover, and there was allegedly some embarrassment in connection with their provision of presses used in making the Mercedes-Benz G-Wagen, which at that time was seen as a Range Rover rival. So the Range Rover business was spun off with the new name of Overfinch. In 1985, Overfinch was sold to new owners, who continued offering a wide range of enhancements for the original Range Rover right up to the end of its production in 1996 – and beyond.

Schuler and Overfinch Range Rovers were always expensive, and that ensured their rarity. But there was always a ready demand from wealthy buyers for these high-performance Range Rovers, and in that demand can be seen the origins of what became the target market for the Range Rover Sport.

CREATION OF LAND ROVER LTD

Inevitably, British Leyland's problems led to a crisis, and at the end of 1974 the car maker had to seek government support to prevent total collapse. The government stepped in with money, and immediately began to investigate ways of returning British Leyland to profit. The Land Rover products had been consistent profit earners, and the important decision was made to turn Land Rover into a standalone business unit, and to manage it separately from the Rover car marque. So in 1978 Land Rover Ltd was created, with a substantial financial investment from the government.

British Leyland's subsequent unhappy history needs no retelling here, but it is important to remember that it was during the 1980s that the Range Rover was moved resolutely up-market to become a proper luxury car (without losing the off-road abilities that it had inherited from the Land Rover). In this decade, it was largely the success of the Range Rover that persuaded Japanese companies to introduce cheaper equivalents aimed at family buyers, and it was the success of these that led Land Rover to introduce the Discovery as a competitor in 1989.

BMW BUYS THE ROVER GROUP

Fast forward now to the 1990s. Land Rover Ltd still belonged to British Leyland (known as the Rover Group since 1986), still had three product lines, and was thriving. The Rover Group as a whole, however, was not. It had passed out of government ownership to British Aerospace in 1988, and that company had somewhat reluctantly agreed to manage it

The Land Rover Discovery was introduced in 1989 and gave Land Rover its third model range. This is the very first production model.

The Freelander became Land Rover's fourth model range in 1997, giving the company a smaller and less expensive entry-level passenger-carrying model. This is the three-door model; a five-door proved more popular with family buyers.

for a period of five years. As soon as those five years were up, BAe scouted around for a buyer, and in 1994 the whole Rover Group was sold to the German car maker BMW.

BMW were good for Land Rover. They improved build quality and supported the company's plan to introduce a fourth product line, which became the Freelander compact SUV in 1997. By this time, passenger-carrying Land Rovers were being built in far greater numbers than the original commercial models (rebranded Defenders in 1990), and the company's outlook was gradually changing. It was at this point that ideas for what would eventually become the Range Rover Sport began to surface – although it would be several years before they became reality.

PROJECT HEARTLAND, 1994–1997

Land Rover was already thinking about the model that would replace its hugely successful Discovery by the time BMW took control in 1994. Project Tempest was really a cautious evolution of the original vehicle, and BMW encouraged the Land Rover teams to be more ambitious in their thinking. So although they allowed the Tempest programme to continue, the Germans persuaded Land Rover to start work on a far more radical alternative. This programme was run in parallel with Project Tempest, and the Discovery it was designed to deliver could have replaced Tempest as the second-generation production model if things had turned out differently.

Fundamental to the more radical Discovery concept was input from Wolfgang Reitzle, the BMW advanced engineering chief who had been appointed to run the Rover Group. He pointed out that imported vehicles sold well in the coastal areas of the USA but not so well in the middle of the country. He pushed for the future Discovery to hit Jeep sales in this heartland area of the USA, and so the project acquired its name of Heartland.

There was no doubt that Heartland would have to be bigger than the existing and planned second-generation Discoverys if it was to meet US market expectations, and its seven-seat accommodation would have to be better and more flexible than that of either vehicle. John Hall, who had run the programme to deliver the second-generation Range Rover and had now been appointed to run the Heartland project, remembered that the size of the Heartland vehicle became a key issue as a result. What US customers wanted would seem very big to Europeans, while a European-size vehicle was too small to meet US requirements.

The L35 and L36

So the compromise solution was to develop two versions, a short-wheelbase five-seater aimed primarily but not exclusively at the European market, and a long-wheelbase seven-seater aimed primarily (but again, not exclusively) at the US market. These two related projects gained the code names of

L35 and L36 respectively, using the new project code system that BMW had introduced. The exact size of Heartland was never firmly settled, but George Thomson, who was leading the Design Studio input to the project, remembered that the shorter wheelbase would have been between 2,642 and 2,692mm (104 and 106in), while the longer one would have added 100 to 120mm (some 4 to 5in) to that. A longer rear overhang on the seven-seater would have allowed the spare wheel to be stowed under the floor, while on the five-seater it would have been carried outside.

However, other issues came to bear on the Heartland project. First of all, BMW decided not to go ahead with the major Range Rover facelift that Land Rover had planned for the 1999 model-year, but instead to put additional resources into getting an all-new Range Rover on the market about three years after that. Then there was the fact that BMW themselves were working in an on-off fashion on their own SUV model, which they knew as the E53 project and which would become the BMW X5 when it was released in 1999. As a BMW, it inevitably had a strong dose of sportiness in its make-up. On top of all that, the CB40 (Freelander) project was consuming a lot of money and engineering resources. So in early 1997 Heartland, in its initial L35 and L36 guise, was cancelled, and Land Rover's original plan to make the Tempest vehicle into the new Discovery was carried forward to production. It became the Discovery Series II in 1998.

THE NEXT STAGE: PROJECTS L50 AND L51

Nevertheless, the work that had gone into Project Heartland was not lost. Some of the thinking that had gone into it was carried through to similar twin projects, known as L50 and L51. These two were again intended to deliver five-seater and seven-seater versions of a new Discovery, but this time the five-seater was not aimed primarily at Europe, but was partly a response to pressure from the USA, where Land Rover North America (LRNA) wanted what was in effect a smaller Discovery with a flat roof – 'a sort of Discovery Sport', as Land Rover designer Dave Saddington later explained it: 'The seven-seater had a clear business case but nobody could nail down any sales volumes for the five-seater. It was going to be first into a new market.'

Using monocoque construction to build two different models was considered to be too complicated and expensive. So the plan quickly gelled around the idea of using a

Project Heartland would have delivered a more sophisticated and refined new Discovery. This sketch proposal was produced in 1994.

BELOW: **These two full-size models are L50 and L51 as they looked in 1999; the five-seat model with the flat roof on the right was intended to be the sportier design for the USA. These are the origins of the Range Rover Sport.**

separate chassis – although the load-bearing function could be shared to some extent by the body so that the chassis could be more lightly constructed. An important issue was that L50 and L51 were going to have beam axles, because BMW wanted them to be down-market of their own X5 with its all-independent suspension, and also because beam axles gave better off-road performance, which would be expected of a Land Rover. Once the idea of using a separate chassis was in place, a plan surfaced to use yet another version of this chassis for a new Defender as well – although that would never come to fruition.

Everything then changed again in summer 2000, when BMW sold Land Rover to Ford. Although L50 and L51

continued to exist for another few months, Land Rover's new owners lost no time in getting to grips with their latest acquisition and in reviewing Land Rover's future model plans. And although nobody realized it at the time, in the five-seater Discovery that had been part of the programme lay the spark that would later ignite as the Range Rover Sport.

The Significance of the Sport

The rest of the Range Rover Sport story forms the remaining chapters of this book, but before getting into detail it is instructive to look at what the Sport did for Land Rover.

When the Sport was introduced in 2005, it was Land Rover's fifth model line. Three of the others (the Range Rover, Discovery and Freelander) were passenger-carrying models; only the Defender was fundamentally a commercial vehicle, but even that was increasingly being bought in Station Wagon form for passenger-carrying duties. So Land Rover's transition from a maker of utility vehicles to a maker of specialized passenger-carrying types was already well under way.

What the Range Rover Sport did was to tip the balance still further towards passenger carriers. But as Land Rover's entry into a new and emerging market for what the Americans had branded as performance SUVs (Sport Utility Vehicles), it required some mental adjustment at Solihull. Although there was a worldwide appreciation of the Land Rover marque, this was something new and different. It added sportiness, style and fashion into the traditional Land Rover mix, and it was the job of the marketing and public

By the mid-2000s, the original Land Rover had evolved into the Land Rover Defender, and passenger-carrying Station Wagons, like this one, had become very popular. This was the well-equipped 110 XS Station Wagon, at the top of the range from October 2002.

Other makers had spotted the market for a sporty SUV that could also be used as a family vehicle. This was BMW's X5, which reached the market in 1999.
VAUXFORD/WIKIMEDIA COMMONS

Aimed at very much the same market was the Porsche Cayenne, which made its appearance in 2002. At the time, many people ridiculed the idea of a sports car manufacturer trying to make an SUV, but they were wrong...
OSX/WIKIMEDIA COMMONS

relations teams to ensure that these new elements blended seamlessly into public expectations, as well as winning over new customers.

Their success was unquestionable. Although (as noted earlier) there was some resistance from traditional Land Rover owners who felt that the Sport deviated too far from the Land Rover norm, the model's success was extraordinarily rapid. Released in 2005, it became Land Rover's best seller for 2006, and in a distant echo of the original 1948 Land Rover's story, it went on to exceed the expectations of its manufacturers. Initially envisaged as a fashionable model that would need regular changes to remain fresh, and which might have a limited production life, it actually lasted for eight and a half years. And in that time, it taught Land Rover a great deal about brand values and premium marketing – lessons that the company continues to use to good effect.

EARLY DESIGN AND DEVELOPMENT

Things moved very quickly once Ford had taken over control of Land Rover in summer 2000. The American company put in their own Steve Ross as Land Rover's new engineering chief, and by the autumn there were serious discussions about the way forward. Decisions were quickly taken about key issues, and one of them was that the reliance on BMW engines had to end. Future Land Rover engines were to come from Jaguar, who had of course been in the Ford stable for many years already, and from other Ford-owned sources.

What BMW had known as the L50 and L51 projects were still in existence, but not surprisingly the BMW engineer who had been running them was recalled to Munich. Into the breach as caretaker manager stepped John Hall, who was then in charge of Advanced Vehicle Design. Hall inherited a project that was becoming stale: there were still multiple unresolved issues about costings, and over in the Design Studio run by Geoff Upex there was a similar sense of staleness. Designer Dave Saddington sensed it keenly, and he felt that the problem lay in the perception of the smaller, five-seat model. So he tried an experiment, positioning one of the full-size L50 models between a Range Rover and an existing production Discovery, and masking off some elements of the design with black tape to suggest a new approach to the five-seater model. 'I tried to get people to think of it as a baby Range Rover rather than as a Discovery minus,' he explained some years later.

THE L319 AND L320 PROJECTS

It was an approach that rapidly gained approval, not only within the design team, but also in the wider company beyond. Thinking of the new vehicle as a baby Range Rover 'automatically put it into a higher price bracket, so there was no longer any need to bring it down to a price. That made for a better business case!' So instead of two variants of the Discovery, Ford authorized work on the related L319 and L320 projects. L319 became the Discovery 3 (LR3 in the USA) on its release in 2004, and L320 became the Range Rover Sport when it was released a year later.

There was still no reason why L319 and L320 should not share a common platform, and in fact Ford took the idea one step further. At some time in the future Land Rover would have to develop a replacement for the long-running Defender range, and Ford envisaged that this could have yet another variant or variants of the new platform. An option that seemed to have considerable promise was to use the

Geoff Upex ran the Land Rover Design Studio in the first half of the 2000s, and the design 'language' used on the models of that period was largely his creation.

chassis of the then unreleased new Ford Explorer (model U152) as that new platform. Land Rover's new engineering chief Steve Ross was probably in favour of the idea, not least because he had led the Ford programme to develop it!

However, neither Ford headquarters at Dearborn nor Steve Ross in Britain had any intention of imposing ideas on the Land Rover engineers willy-nilly. So in September 2000, a group of Land Rover's chassis and packaging engineers flew out to Ford engineering headquarters in Dearborn for a three-month period in which they were to examine this option in detail. They were headed by Steve Haywood, who had run the engineering teams for the first Land Rover Freelander in the mid-1990s and had then been seconded to a Rover cars project (called R30) that was being run from BMW headquarters in Munich. That project was cancelled when BMW sold Rover Cars, and Steve transferred back to Land Rover.

After some careful debate, the Dearborn study group reached the conclusion that the Explorer's separate chassis would not be suitable for future Land Rovers. Some years later Steve Haywood remembered:

It was too low to the ground. The approach and departure angles were inadequate, and there was insufficient suspension travel. So it would have needed too much new hardware. We also studied the interior package, and the 'command driving position' just wasn't there. Those two fundamentals were too far from the brand DNA, and the platform was too important for Land Rover's future. So we convinced management that we needed a new platform.

A New Chassis

Steve and his team quickly conceived that new platform as a separate chassis – a conservative approach by comparison with the huge monocoque that BMW had approved for the L322 Range Rover, but considerably cheaper and more flexible. Even so, the new chassis was certainly not going to be a conventional design. Instead, it was to be much lighter than Land Rover chassis of old, and was to carry an ultra-rigid monocoque bodyshell that would bear a proportion of the loads that had traditionally been carried solely by the chassis. When this idea was brought to market with the new Discovery in 2004, it was given the name of 'integrated body-frame construction' – partly to explain how it worked, but also undoubtedly to make it sound more exciting than it really was.

During December 2000, the new strategy fell into place. Steve Haywood remembered visiting Dearborn that month to make what Ford call the 'strategic intent presentation' to the then outgoing Chairman, Jac Nasser. The next twelve

Ford were understandably keen to use the platform of their latest Explorer, coded U152, for the new generation of Land Rovers – but it quickly became clear that this was not going to work.
IFCAR/WIKIMEDIA COMMONS

Steve Haywood was appointed to run the T5 chassis development team, and later took charge of the L319 project that delivered the Discovery 3.

months would see the rest of the engineering and design come together.

So the Land Rover engineers now had the job of designing and developing a new lightweight chassis that would suit the L319 Discovery, the L320 baby Range Rover and, longer term, the Defender replacement. This was probably known as L321, a programme number otherwise unaccounted for – although Land Rover have never confirmed this, and the programme never became reality. The new chassis took on another new Ford codename and became T5. Just one important design element survived from Land Rover's brush with the Explorer: this was the 'portholes' in the rear chassis side members, which allowed the driveshafts to run through, rather than under, the chassis rails.

Quite early on in the T5 programme the designers realized that the chassis they wanted could not be manufactured using the traditional die-stamping process. They needed quite complex shapes to get the high stiffness-to-weight ratio that was in the plan, and the only way to achieve these was to use the relatively new process of hydroforming. This used water under high pressure to mould metal into the required shape: the blank metal was placed inside a die of the intended shape, and high-pressure water injected behind the metal to force it into the die. Unfortunately there was as yet no plant in the UK where a hydroformed structure as big as the T5 chassis frame could be manufactured.

This was where association with a huge company such as Ford had its merits. The guarantee of large volumes enabled Ford to persuade GKN in the UK, and what was then the Dana Corporation of the USA, to establish a joint venture to build it. The new company was called Chassis Systems Ltd, and in 2002 work began on its new factory in Telford. This was the Dana Corporation's first hydroforming business in Europe; production began in 2003, and the T5 chassis frames for the L319 Discovery and L320 baby Range Rover were built there using Dana's patented Robo Clamp process. An additional advantage of hydroforming was that it was actually less expensive than traditional die-stamping.

The first T5 chassis prototypes did not, of course, have the benefit of being made in the new plant. They were instead built rather more laboriously and by hand, and were ready by summer 2001. Land Rover knew them as 'Attribute Prototypes' (a term used for prototypes that incorporate proposed elements of a future vehicle), and some were for L320 while others were for L319. They took to the roads for testing straightaway in the form of 'mules', disguised under the bodies of Ford Explorers and Mercury Mountaineers. Although some members of the press realized that they must be test prototypes, it was impossible to tell exactly what was being tested without getting close to the vehicle for a detailed examination – and Land Rover took great care to ensure that could never happen.

Prototypes of the T5 chassis were disguised with the bodies of Ford Explorers and Mercury Mountaineers. This 'Mountaineer' was pictured during off-road testing in February 2003.
JAN PRINS

DYNAMIC RESPONSE

The suspension system that Land Rover called 'Dynamic Response' was a specially developed compact version of the 'active stabilizer bar system', designed and manufactured by Delphi Energy & Chassis Systems, an American company whose UK headquarters were in Luton. It was developed jointly by the two companies, and Land Rover's L320 vehicle became its first production application.

Dynamic Response replaced traditional anti-roll bars with bars that were split in the middle. At this mid-point, computer-controlled rotary actuators applied a variable level of torque, based on inputs from two lateral accelerometers and a steering angle sensor. In corners, roll stiffness was instantly increased by applying torque to the appropriate bar.

By contrast, when the vehicle was travelling in a straight line, the anti-roll bars were in effect decoupled, so improving ride comfort. In off-road use, the same decoupling of the anti-roll bars allowed large wheel articulation to the benefit of grip and traction.

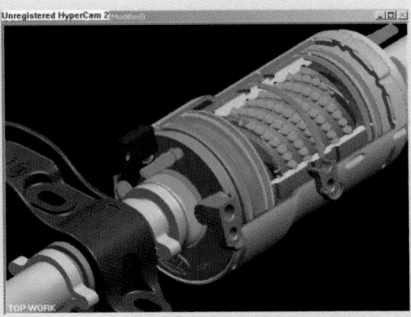

Land Rover and Delphi developed new, compact rotary actuators for the split anti-roll bars of the Dynamic Response system.

The main difference between the L319 and L320 Attribute Prototypes was that those for L320 had their suspension tuned to give more sporty characteristics. In its early stages was the ARM system, those letters standing for 'active roll mitigation', and the system itself being a further development of ACE ('active cornering enhancement'), already in production for the Discovery Series II. ACE pioneered the use of accelerometers mounted high up in the vehicle body to detect the onset of roll in a corner, and to instruct hydraulic rams to stiffen the effect of the anti-roll bars. ARM would become part of the Dynamic Response suspension system that was new for L320, and would be standard only on top models.

IT'S A RANGE ROVER

Richard Woolley, who headed the Design Studio team that worked on the vehicle, recalls October 2001 as being the date when the L320 programme kicked off in earnest. The basics of the T5 platform had been settled, and the L319 and L320 programmes had been formally separated, Steve Haywood changed jobs to become Chief Programme Engineer for L319, and Tom Jones was appointed as the Chief Programme Engineer for L320. Nevertheless, the two programmes would always remain linked because of the plan for them to share as much hardware as possible. In fact there would be a much higher proportion of shared components than most buyers of either vehicle would ever appreciate.

While the focus had been on designing the T5 chassis, some preliminary work had been going ahead on both vehicles. For the L320, the benchmarks were seen as the BMW X5, the Porsche Cayenne, and some derivatives of the Mercedes-Benz ML-class, the three models that had created a new market sector for sporty SUV models. However, it was also clear that L320 had to have Range Rover characteristics. It was not to be a competitor for the existing Range Rover, but rather to package most of the Range Rover qualities and characteristics to suit a different target audience. From early on, the key L320 quality was that it was to be sporty and exciting, while the existing Range Rover remained grand and aloof. This distinction also helped to define the boundaries of the L319 and L320 programmes. L320 was expected to stand between the Range Rover and the Discovery in the Land Rover hierarchy.

Size was also to help define the differences between L319 and L320. Following on from the thinking that had gone into L50 and L51 earlier, the L319 Discovery needed a 2,896mm (114in) wheelbase to make room for its three rows of

Richard Woolley was the Studio Director with responsibility for the design of L320.

Considering L320 as a variety of Range Rover had important ramifications in many areas. Land Rover's marketing people had to create for it a distinctive image that would prevent it from damaging sales of the 'full-size' Range Rover, and everything that the designers and engineers working on the development programme did also had to align with that image. It implied a high degree of luxury, of sophistication, and of style, and all of that had to be wrapped up with new levels of sportiness and driving dynamics. Creating L320 in a three-year time-frame was going to be a serious challenge.

SUSPENSION, STEERING AND BRAKES

Land Rovers, Discoverys and Range Rovers had all relied on beam axles until the turn of the century, and the only product from Solihull that had independent suspension was the Freelander, introduced as a 1998 model. It was a core Land Rover belief that beam axles gave far better off-road performance than independent suspension, although the benefits of independent suspension for on-road use were unquestionable. The Freelander had excellent off-road ability for its class, but was well known to be inferior to the bigger Land Rovers off-road, in spite of help from some sophisticated electronic traction aids.

However, all that was about to change. Well aware that the Range Rover could not provide a fully credible challenge to conventional luxury cars if it continued to rely on beam axles, Land Rover were planning to introduce all-round independent suspension on the new L322 Range Rover. In conjunction with air springs – already pioneered on beam-axled Range Rovers – this would give the necessary high levels of ride comfort and on-road handling. However, it would also rely on sophisticated electronics to retain the off-road abilities of a beam-axled vehicle.

Briefly, the issue was this: in rough going, the wheels of a vehicle are often pushed up into the wheel-arches; with beam axles, as one wheel goes up, the one on the opposite end of the axle goes down, helping to maintain tyre contact and traction. With independent suspension, it is possible for both wheels at one end to be pushed up at the same time, perhaps grounding the vehicle in the centre. So for L322, an electronic control system 'cross-linked' the air-suspension units when low range was selected for off-road driving, making each pair of wheels behave as if they were linked by a

seats. L320, by contrast, continued the thinking about the smaller, five-seat model, and so its wheelbase was settled as 2,743mm (108in) – 152mm (6in) shorter than the Discovery, and – perhaps not entirely coincidentally – the same size as the second-generation Range Rover then in production. The new L322 Range Rover, which would be announced at the end of 2001, had meanwhile been designed with a wheelbase of 2,880mm (113.4in) (Land Rover engineers actually worked in metric dimensions).

There was as yet no formal decision about what the new model should be called, although the focus on sporting qualities quickly led to the use of 'Range Rover Sport' as an unofficial description. Others at Land Rover continued to call it the 'Baby Range Rover'. It would be three years or more before 'Range Rover Sport' was finally chosen as the name for the production models.

beam axle, so providing optimum tyre contact and traction while minimizing the risk of grounding.

From a very early stage, the engineers working on the T5 chassis pushed hard for independent suspension instead of beam axles. 'We were about enhancing off-road and vastly improving on-road,' remembered Steve Haywood. So the T5 team were given access to the new technology being developed for the L322 Range Rover, and drew up their own all-independent suspension system that combined this with double-wishbone suspension hardware at each wheel station. As a result, L320 (and, of course, L319) would have Land Rover's traditional superb off-road ability, and both ride and handling that were directly comparable to saloon cars, with which it would compete.

Special attention was also given to steering to get the crisp on-road handling that was needed, in particular for L320. The plan was to use a power-assisted rack-and-pinion system, and to mount it carefully so that the vicious kickback that such systems typically produced in rough terrain did not become a problem. However, the system originally chosen proved too quick at speed, and did not have the required agility at low speeds, and so this was changed quite late in the development programme, after the first full prototypes had been built in 2003. Stuart Frith, then running the Prototype Development department at Gaydon, knew from his work on Jaguar projects that ZF could deliver to fairly short time-scales, and suggested that the German company should be asked to come up with a suitable variable-ratio, speed-

proportional, power-assisted rack-and-pinion system. The ZF proposal, a version of their Servotronic system, was adopted for production.

The braking system was built on existing Land Rover practice, with four-wheel disc brakes that had servo assistance, and an ABS system that worked both on and off the road. There were some important novelties, however. Just about to be introduced on the L322 Range Rover was a new type of handbrake mechanism that worked on drums incorporated within the rear discs. This replaced the transmission brake traditional to Land Rovers, and prevented the 'lurch' associated with those types if the vehicle was parked on a hill. It was a natural choice for the new models with the T5 chassis.

Also new was an electronic handbrake system that had been developed by Jaguar. Instead of a traditional handbrake lever, this worked by means of a small paddle switch, which freed up space on the transmission tunnel and allowed the designers to produce a more aesthetically pleasing interior. The switch applied the handbrake by means of a servo motor, and disengaged it too – although there was also a system that disengaged it automatically as the vehicle moved away from rest. Successful in Jaguars, this system would go on to give a fair amount of trouble in Land Rover products in the beginning.

One more new feature was introduced specifically for the L320 versions of the T5 chassis. In the plan was an ultra-high performance derivative (which would have the supercharged engine described below), and this was going to need brakes that were more powerful than standard. So for this variant, the T5 engineers decided to use four-piston brake callipers made by the Italian specialist Brembo, with larger-diameter discs on all four wheels.

THE TERRAIN RESPONSE SYSTEM

As Land Rover products became increasingly sophisticated and refined, they also attracted a different group of buyers, and so the company established a market research programme to keep abreast of changes in its target buyers' tastes and perceptions. From this programme, it became clear that buyers of even the most luxurious models were unwilling to sacrifice the off-road capability associated with the Land Rover name, but that they would appreciate simpler controls for the hardware that made it possible. Many

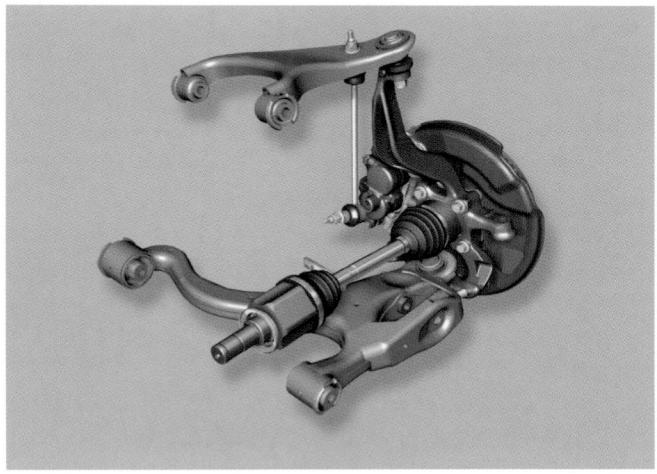

All-round independent front suspension was central to the T5 chassis design. This is the twin-wishbone design that was used on the front wheels.

were also well aware that they had not developed the skills to enable them to become competent off-road drivers.

Land Rover acted on this knowledge in several different ways, but there was one way that became an important part of the T5 chassis development programme. This was the design and development of a computer-aided off-road driving system that co-ordinated the vehicle's systems to provide the best possible traction in different circumstances. The idea was to remove from the driver the responsibility for decisions that needed skill as well as judgement.

Jan Prins, a Dutch engineer who had come to work for Land Rover, led the team that developed the new system. It became known as Terrain Response, and in production would be operated by a rotary control on the centre console of the vehicle: turning the control to one of a series of icons gave the optimum vehicle response for the type of ground selected. So the accelerator, suspension, gearbox, brakes, 'Hill Descent Control' and traction control systems responded differently in 'rock crawl' mode from the way

Ease of use was an important design criterion for L320, and Terrain Response was operated by a simple rotary control on the centre console.

they responded in 'mud and ruts' mode or in 'general driving' mode. The whole system was dependent on the latest data bus technology that linked the various systems involved, and co-ordinated their actions to deliver the best possible traction in different circumstances.

Terrain Response was a superb achievement, but it had, of course, been developed as part of the T5 chassis programme and was therefore specifically intended to work with that chassis. As a result, it was introduced on the models with that chassis – L319 first, and L320 a year later – and it was not until a year after its appearance on L320 that it also became available on Land Rover's L322 flagship model.

ENGINE DEVELOPMENT

Ford obviously wanted Land Rover to stop using BMW engines as soon as possible. Not only was the German company a rival manufacturer, but appropriate engines could be supplied from within the Ford family of companies for much lower cost. So the engines strategy for L320 was developed as part of a wider strategy that included replacement engines for the L322 Range Rover, and of course, engines for the planned new L319 Discovery.

The obvious source of a new V8 petrol engine to replace the BMW 4.4-litre type in L322 was Jaguar. The company's AJ-V8 design was still relatively new, having been introduced in 1996, and although all existing production derivatives had capacities of 4.0 litres or less, Jaguar was working on a 4.2-litre block for its next version of the engine. Land Rover's

Jan Prins was the engineer behind Land Rover's groundbreaking Terrain Response traction system.

ABOVE: **All three engines for L320 came from the Jaguar stable. This cutaway shows the 4.4-litre petrol V8 that was central to the range of options...**

marketing teams felt that using an engine of smaller capacity than the BMW would look like a step backwards, and so the engine designers were instructed to develop a 4.4-litre block from the 4.2-litre size. A bore increase of 2mm did the trick, wrapped up as part of the programme to make the engine suitable for Land Rover vehicles – where off-road use places unique demands on such things as oil and cooling systems, as well as waterproofing.

The name AJ-V8 stood for 'Advanced Jaguar V8', and the basic engine was an all-alloy, four-camshaft design with 4 valves per cylinder. It was manufactured in a dedicated Jaguar facility located inside Ford's engine plant at Bridgend in South Wales, and replaced both the long-serving Jaguar V12 engine and the 6-cylinder AJ6 family. The Land Rover version of the engine produced 300bhp – more than the 290bhp of the Jaguar 4.2-litre engine, and also more than the BMW 4.4-litre engine could muster. It was going to be ideal as the core petrol engine for L320.

However, the planning did not stop there. The 4.2-litre V8 would be accompanied by a supercharged version when it entered production in 2002 for Jaguar's own cars, and this presented very interesting possibilities for Land Rover. A

... and this one shows the supercharged version of the engine that was chosen for use in the top models of L320.

23

In this picture of the 2.7-litre TDV6 engine, the deep sump designed specifically for Land Rover use is very obvious.

supercharged V8 sounded like exactly the sort of engine that would give L320 a distinctive performance orientation, and it would also be ideal for a flagship version of the L322 Range Rover, which had been intended to have a BMW V12 engine in its top models, but of course would not do so now that Ford owned the company.

So the 4.2-litre supercharged V8 was also given an overhaul to suit use in a vehicle designed to spend time off-road, and it emerged with a power output of 390bhp – vastly more than any production Land Rover had ever had, even though it sounds quite tame by more recent standards.

With the naturally aspirated V8 taking care of the middle of the range, and the supercharged version selected to power the flagship variants of L320, the next job was to find a suitable diesel engine. This would be vital in Europe, where diesel power dominated and large petrol engines were relatively unpopular. Once again, Jaguar came to the rescue, this time with the 2.7-litre V6 diesel that had come about as part of a Ford project run jointly with PSA Peugeot-Citroën in France.

That project had begun with the signing of a joint development agreement in 1998, known as the Gemini project. Ford and Peugeot-Citroën agreed to develop a whole family of diesel engines, and within that family (which were otherwise 4-cylinder types) was to be a turbocharged V6 engine suitable for installation in Peugeot and Citroën models while also being suitable for north-south installation in Jaguars. The result was a world-class multi-valve twin overhead cam-shaft diesel engine with a cylinder block made of compacted graphite iron. It made its debut in Jaguar's XJ saloons in 2.7-litre form with twin turbochargers. Ford and Jaguar called it the Lion V6.

Land Rover's engineers redeveloped it, of course, this time not for the L322 Range Rover, but for L320 and for the L319 Discovery. They redesigned the sump and improved water and dust sealing, added a larger fan to improve cooling for off-road use, and fitted a single turbocharger in place of Jaguar's two in order to improve low-speed torque for towing and off-road work. What Land Rover called the TDV6 would always be built alongside Jaguar versions of the engine at Ford's Dagenham engine plant; the Peugeot-Citroën versions were meanwhile built at Douvrin and Trémery in France.

GEARBOXES

Two things were clear from the beginning. One was that L320 was a Land Rover product and would therefore have to have a transfer gearbox with low-range gears to provide the traditional Land Rover off-road ability. The other was that if it was to be a luxury vehicle along the lines of the Range Rover (note that the use of Range Rover in its name had not yet been decided), it would have to have an automatic gearbox as standard. In practice, a manual option seems to have been ruled out early on.

Land Rover had been using automatic gearboxes built by ZF in Germany since the mid-1980s, and there was no good reason to change supplier. The latest ZF offering suitable for the power and torque outputs of the planned engines was a six-speed type, giving smaller increments between gears than earlier designs and therefore smoother functioning. Both fifth and sixth ratios were geared as overdrives, which aided refinement and fuel consumption in high-speed cruising. Known as the 6HP26, this gearbox was chosen for use with all three planned engines.

The drive from this gearbox would be split between the front and rear pairs of wheels by a two-speed transfer gearbox, which in the Land Rover tradition would have a high ratio for everyday driving and a low ratio giving greater control and more hauling power for off-road work. Traditionally, the high and low ratios had been selected manually by an additional control lever, but it was now a Range Rover tradition to use servo motors to do the actual selection of

The two-speed transfer box chosen was a silent, chain-driven type manufactured by Magna Steyr. This cutaway example shows its interior design.

gears, and either micro-switches on the selector lever or a separate switch on the dashboard to activate them. As L320 was being aligned with the Range Rover brand, it would obviously need some form of electric actuation.

Interestingly, the engineers working on L319 and L320 decided against using the US-made New Venture NV225 transfer box then planned for the L322 Range Rover. Perhaps they had some inkling that it would prove troublesome in service (its weaknesses turned out to be failure of the front propshaft splines and stretching of the Hy-Vo drive chain). Instead, they chose a transfer box made by Magna Steyr in Austria and known as the DD295 type. The DD295 was another chain-driven gearbox, this time with a bevel gear differential that normally split torque 50:50 front to rear, but it also had a multi-plate clutch pack that could vary that torque distribution and also lock the centre differential. This proved highly satisfactory – and in mid-2005 was adopted for the L322 as well to replace the earlier type of transfer box. Land Rover generally referred to it as the D7u type.

EXTERIOR DESIGN

Immediately after the Ford takeover of Land Rover, Geoff Upex had been appointed as head of the Land Rover Design Studio – the department that had once been known as

Styling. Under him were individual studio directors, perhaps best understood as team leaders, and from among them he chose Richard Woolley to lead the team that would work up the body design for L320. Woolley had earlier been with the cars side of the Rover Group, where he had overseen design of the highly acclaimed Rover 75 saloon released in 1998. 'Our brief was to create an all-new product for Land Rover that embodied Range Rover style in a more compact, sporty package,' he remembered later.

The initial design sketches for L320 were done in late 2000, before the engineering programme started in earnest. Among them were some by Mike Sampson, which envisaged L320 as a two-door model with a number of design cues from the very first Range Rover of 1970. These included edge-pull door handles, a clamshell bonnet, and even a mock-up of the twin fans behind the grille! Richard Woolley believed that the two-door configuration 'could epitomise the sporty aspect I was looking for, and help reinforce L320's individuality among its stablemates.'

Nevertheless, the two-door idea did not last long. Customer research fed into the L320 programme made quite clear that buyers wanted a four-door layout, and so the programme embraced that. But this was to be a very different kind of Land Rover product, and so Mike Sampson proposed what he called a one-and-a-half door layout for each side. There would be a long front door, to give the appearance of a sporty coupé, with a rear-hinged half-size back door. This looked like a flyer for a time, and in fact an engineering

The two-door proposal was worked up into a full-size clay model, pictured here under construction in the Design Studio.

By the time it was completed, the two-door clay was wearing 'Range Sport' decals on its nose. It looks a little ungainly here, not least because the far side of the model is longer and showcases an alternative design. The front end combines the vertical-bar grille of the original Range Rover with the latest front lamp unit design of overlapping circles.

Early thoughts by designer Mike Sampson were to make L320 into a two-door, complete with edge-pull door handles like the original 1970 Range Rover. Mike was one of those who favoured the Range Rover Sport name from the start.

package prototype was built on the chassis of a second-generation Range Rover.

However, the idea was not pursued. 'The major problem was building enough strength into the body,' according to Mike Sampson. 'It was too risky, and would have been too

When customer clinics showed a marked preference for four doors, Mike Sampson drew up this pillarless 'one-and-a-half-door' proposal.

This proposal came very early in the programme if we are to believe the date of 2000 on it.

high an investment for the then predicted volumes.' So the design team went back to a conventional four-door configuration during 2001, and this idea was in place before the L320 programme as a whole got into gear in October that year.

Among the elements shared between L320 and L319 were to be large sections of the inner body structure, and to a degree this sharing dictated what the designers could and could not do. It was never a major hindrance, though, and the L320 design came together as a coherent whole, its sporty nature emphasized by a more raked windscreen than

on the forthcoming new Range Rover and by a peak-like rear spoiler at roof level, a feature seen earlier on the Rover 200 hatchback car that had been primarily Dave Saddington's work.

As this was to be a Range Rover, it had to retain Range Rover styling cues, and yet it also had to have what Upex later called an 'aerodynamic and muscular exterior design. It had to look dynamic and exciting, and be utterly tempting. We wanted a muscular, hewn-from-the-solid design that promised great power.'

So all these requirements were combined with established Range Rover features such as the floating roof (achieved by combining a body-colour roof with black window pillars) and clamshell bonnet. A more raked screen angle helped to give

By this stage, L320 was to be a four-door model, but this Mike Sampson sketch shows that the name was still not settled. 'Range Sport' was considered, but did not flow as well as Range Rover Sport.

Bold tail-lights, front wing vents, and a lower tailgate finisher with the Land Rover brand name were all carried over to production, but not in quite the form they appear here.

the necessary sporty look, but in one respect L320 strayed from the established Range Rover norm: a key Range Rover design cue was bonnet castellations, but the design team did not incorporate these in their L320 design. Launch press material suggested that they had been left off to improve airflow, but Geoff Upex's recollection was more honest: 'We wanted a smoother, more aerodynamic look,' he said.

Land Rover had put considerable effort into designing a new 'face' for its twenty-first century models, and an important element in that incorporated headlamp units in which round foglamps intersected round headlamps. So a version of this was integrated into the front end of L320, the lamp units flanking a silver-finished grille with three perforated plastic bars, giving a powerful frontal appearance that was imposing but just short of aggressive.

A further link to the Range Rover family came in the shape of front wing vents, although these were quite different from the 'gills' used on the L322 model. Instead, Richard Woolley's team took its inspiration from the wing vents of the high-performance 2001 Bentley Continental R Le Mans, reasoning that this would be entirely in keeping with the sporty flavour of the new Land Rover model!

The need to be subtly different from the 'full-size' L322 Range Rover also affected the design of the tailgate, although other factors played their part here as well. The tailgate on L322 followed the Range Rover tradition of a horizontal split into two parts, the lower one hinged downwards to make a platform from which such things as country sports could be viewed. However, L320 was aimed at a more urban clientèle, with no obvious need for such a feature, but a very clear need for maximum convenience of use. So for L320 the tailgate was

hinged at the top and lifted upwards on gas struts to give maximum access to the load bay – but it was also designed with a window that could be hinged upwards separately, to provide quick and easy access for small items, such as bags of shopping.

INTERIOR DESIGN

The design of the passenger cabin called for some innovative thinking, because it had to combine Range Rover levels of luxury and finish with a sporting ambience that had never been seen before in any Land Rover product. A further constraint was that the basic architecture of the dashboard could not deviate too far from that of the L319 Discovery, because the two vehicles were to share the same dash armature. The changes had to be made in the foaming on top of that armature, and in the way it was trimmed.

Mark Butler led the interior design for L320. He is pictured here with some interior sketches for LRX, which later became the Range Rover Evoque.

This late sketch by Mike Sampson shows how the production front end would look.

This Mark Butler sketch conveys the high centre console and flowing lines that he wanted to achieve for L320.

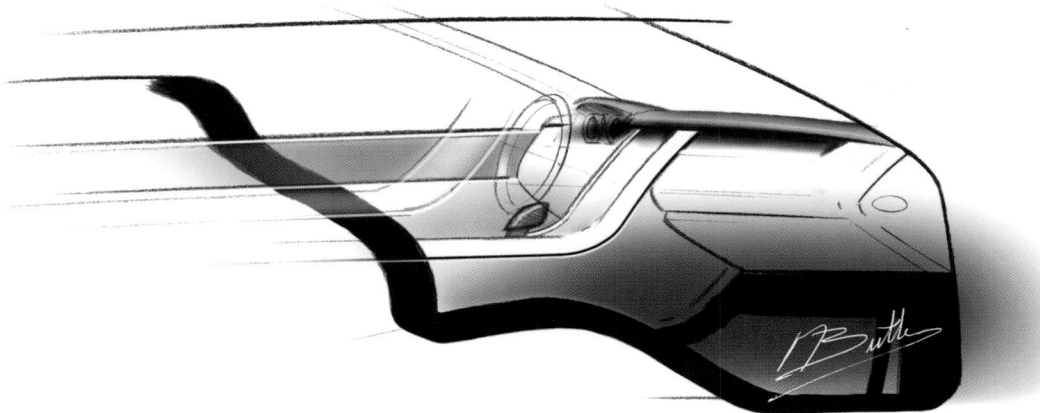

The design was done by Mark Butler and Wyn Thomas, initially purely in CAD, and a full-size clay model was only made later in the process. Their approach was to create a cockpit around the driver, and they achieved this with a high, sweeping centre console that gave a totally different feel from the upright arrangement in L319. The switchgear was mounted much higher than in the typical 4×4, giving a more car-like ambience, and the gear selector was also deliberately offset towards the driver to give a sportier feel. Again this contrasted with the L319 solution, where the selector was centrally placed.

Wood trim (with a silver plastic alternative) along the top edges of the centre console hinted at the wood in the L322 Range Rover and was carried across to unique door cards, while the rectangular air vents in the dash were once again distinctively different from the round ones in L319. Only a close and thoughtful look would reveal the similarities of switchgear and instrumentation, and that the two models shared the same steering wheel. The seats, too, were unique to L320, with a supportive design and sporty look that again emphasized the character of the model.

A NEW ASSEMBLY PLANT

L320 was an incremental product for Land Rover, which joined the Freelander, Defender, Discovery and Range Rover to take the number of distinct models up to five. As a result, new factory space had to be created to assemble it, and Ford chose to redevelop an area of the Solihull factory site for the purpose.

A major new assembly plant was created at the eastern end of the site, where both L319 and L320 would be assembled. This became known as the T5 Trim and Final building ('final' being short for 'final assembly'). There was also huge investment in a new Body In White plant destined to assemble the bodyshells for both models. The first ground for this was broken in July 2002, after a number of older buildings had been demolished. The new assembly areas became operational early in 2004, and initially produced only L319 Discovery 3s, which were introduced around a year before the L320 Range Rover Sport.

CONSTRUCTION OF THE L320 PROTOTYPES

Design work was still in progress when the first prototypes of L320 were constructed in 2001. These were what Land Rover called Attribute Prototypes – in effect 'mules', with some attributes of the planned new vehicle built into existing structures. The T5 chassis prototypes with Explorer and Mountaineer bodies described earlier were simply the first of these.

Full details of all the Attribute Prototypes are not available. However, VU02 RXL was one of them. The 'top hat' mounted on the prototype T5 chassis was the body of a red Mercury Mountaineer. The DVLA records show that it was registered as a Ford in May 2002 and had a 4000cc engine – almost certainly the Ford petrol V6 that would be offered in Discovery 3 (L319) models sold in North America.

The Confirmation Prototypes

The next stage was the construction of Confirmation Prototypes during 2003, using the production body design, chassis and running gear. The L320 programme had been timed so that all the major elements of the new vehicle would have been designed and put through basic testing in time for this, and these were the first prototypes that actually looked like the intended production models. They were hand built by the Prototype Division at Gaydon, the same one that had built and run the T5 chassis 'mules' disguised as Explorers and Mountaineers.

Discovering precise details of prototypes is always tricky, but it looks as if assembly of the Confirmation batch began in July 2003. A total of seventy-two had been built before the end of the year, and a further (unknown) quantity was assembled in April 2004. The first group of forty vehicles was put on the road in October and November 2003, and went out on test immediately afterwards. The known ones had registration plates that made them look older than they were; they had inconspicuous colours, no badges, and rubber

mouldings containing 'slave' headlamp and tail-lamp units. These helped to conceal the shapes actually planned for production, but were probably also necessary because no production units had yet been manufactured!

This first group of forty Confirmation Prototypes were given registration numbers in the sequence V251 HHP to V298 HHP, with some omissions. The V-prefix registrations were normally issued between September 1999 and February 2000, but this batch had not been and was allocated to Land Rover (V299 HHP, incidentally, was allocated to a Discovery 3 prototype). In DVLA records, the make of vehicle was shown as 'Fleet', presumably by special arrangement to maintain security around the L320 project.

The Confirmation Prototypes had special serial numbers, which are shown in Land Rover records as starting with 000500; the highest number so far discovered is 000573, but the numbers certainly continued beyond that. The VINs contained recognizable elements of the production style, but at least one of them was very odd: it is recorded as 1000SALSEAB415A00052 (which was registered as V298 HHP). The real serial number was probably somewhere between 000520 and 000529, and lost its last figure in the recording process.

Most of these vehicles were painted in white, black or silver; a few were green, and one (V251 HHP) was red. The

A Confirmation Prototype pictured on test in the USA. The light units are simply rubber mouldings that contain slave lights, the grille is a dummy, and there is even black masking on the black paint to confuse observers about the real shape. Black fabric covers the distinctive lower door sections, and the wing vent is again a dummy.

Confirmation Prototype V284 HHP pictured during cold-weather tests in Sweden. Once again it has the rubber light units, and this time also a fabric mesh to conceal the grille. Although the wheels are not the ones intended for the top models, it is just possible to see that the front brakes are the Brembo units that were.

V284 HHP again, with the test driver clearly having fun trying out the traction-control systems on snow! The rubber rear lights can be seen here, together with the roof extensions that gave a hint of the Discovery's distinctive outline.

actual body colour was nevertheless often difficult to discern underneath a 'dazzle' type of camouflage that helped to break up the lines of the vehicle when seen at a distance, and so to make spy photography less revealing. Some vehicles also had dummy roof extensions above each body side to suggest the stepped roof of a Discovery.

The Confirmation Prototypes were designed to do exactly what their name suggested: to confirm that the design was satisfactory and ready for production. So they went out on test, and their programme was arranged to meet a deadline of July 2004, when the first volume-production models would begin to come off the lines at Solihull.

It was just as the first Confirmation Prototypes were being assembled that L320's Chief Programme Engineer, Tom Jones, decided to leave Land Rover. There was a brief interregnum, although without interruption to the test programme that was then under way. Then in summer 2004, Stuart Frith found himself appointed to take Jones's place at the head of the L320 project. He was a natural choice for the job, having been so closely involved with testing the chassis prototypes earlier, and he carried the programme through to the launch of the vehicle.

Testing of the Confirmation Prototypes between autumn 2003 and late spring 2004 was very thorough, and took place in a wide variety of locations. In Britain there was testing at MIRA, at Land Rover's own test track at Gaydon, and around its traditional off-road testing ground

at Eastnor Castle. Hot-weather testing was done in Dubai, South Africa, Australia's Nullarbor Plain and California's Death Valley. Some vehicles went to Canada and Sweden for cold-weather testing and also to fine-tune their performance on ice and snow. The chassis tuning was completed at the Nürburgring and at the Nardo race track in southern Italy. A few spy photographers managed to capture prototypes on film, but by and large the disguise was very successful, and it was hard to see exactly what L320 would look like.

The design was largely on target, but there were some late changes. As explained above, the steering was changed as a result of experience with the first Confirmation Prototypes. Body control was also improved by fine-tuning the body mounts themselves, of which there were ten conventional rubber mounts and four miniature damper units. The final stages involved tuning the dampers and selecting the right tyres to give the on-road characteristics that the L320 team wanted. They worked closely with various tyre manufacturers on this, but Stuart Frith remembered that Continental were particularly good because they were able to turn changes around in five or six weeks, half the time it took other manufacturers.

There are no known survivors of the Confirmation Prototype batch. Most were taken off the road between late 2004 and mid-2005, while the last few perhaps survived until the end of 2005 before being broken up.

Caught on the road close to Land Rover's Gaydon engineering headquarters, V263 HHP was put on the road in October 2003 and was a 4.4-litre V8 model. Theoretically it was painted silver, although the camouflage makes it hard to work out what is the base colour and what is not!

By the time this Confirmation Prototype, a white diesel dating from November 2003, was pictured on the tank testing ground at Bovington, the production headlamps were available.

WHAT SHALL WE CALL IT?

Meanwhile, L320 still had no official name. There seems to have been some resistance within Land Rover to calling it a Range Rover, as that was the company's flagship brand and some people felt it should not be diluted in any way. At one point, Land Rover registered the trademarks RS300 and RS400, which were clearly intended to reflect the (approximate) power outputs of L320's two petrol engines.

Nevertheless, the unofficial name of Range Rover Sport soon gained popularity. Its key advantage was that it was a succinct statement of what L320 was all about. There was also the advantage that the Range Rover name was firmly established and had a resonance that would certainly help sales. But the main sticking point was that word 'Sport'. Accurate and evocative though it was, it represented a completely new departure for Land Rover, and there were fears that the buying public might not accept it.

As a result, Land Rover mounted a major campaign to sensitize the public in advance of the new model. The first sign of this was in September 2003, when the facelifted 2004-model Freelander was introduced with the option of a new sports suspension and 18in alloy wheels that earned it the name of Freelander Sport – the word 'Sport' being carried in highly visible decals that ran across the front doors and wings.

The Range Stormer

The next stage was even more ambitious, and involved the creation of a special show car or concept model that was to be displayed in public a year before the Range Rover Sport actually went on sale. Called the Range Stormer, it was not an early concept for the Range Rover Sport, despite what some commentators have suggested. As Geoff Upex told Nick Hull for *Land Rover Design*: 'It wasn't about the production Range Rover Sport, it was about the Range Rover brand....We did it to show to the public that this brand isn't what you think it is, it actually has this other capability of on-road dynamics too.'

Designer Richard Woolley, who oversaw its production, has confirmed that 'the main intention of the Range Stormer was to gauge public reaction to the idea of a sporty Range Rover.' Thus it was deliberately built as a standalone project, an eye-catching show car, as part of the plan to sensitize the public to the idea that a Range Rover could have dynamic road performance.

The Range Stormer was a massive success when it was revealed by Land Rover's Managing Director Matthew Taylor in a dramatic piece of theatre at the Detroit Motor Show in January 2004. 'In the end it had more coverage than any other car at Detroit,' Geoff Upex told Nick Hull.

Work on the show car began in May 2003 and was led by Richard Woolley, Studio Director for the real Range Rover Sport, which had already been signed off for production by that stage. To save time, it was built on the chassis of an old-model (second-generation) Range Rover with left-hand drive, shortened to give a 2,700mm (106.3in) wheelbase. The Range Stormer actually had a 4.6-litre V8 engine, and was drivable to the extent that was necessary for a show car.

Design was completed very quickly, and a full-size clay model was ready by August. The exterior design was led by Sean Henstridge with Paul Hanstock in support, and deliberately exaggerated some of the ideas that had gone into L320. However, the Range Stormer was designed with just two doors rather than the four of the production model – doors that were very special indeed, and were designed to add some drama to the 'reveal' at Detroit. Each door was in two sections, split horizontally: the top section opened up scissor-fashion, and the lower section folded down to provide an entrance step. The whole system was operated by hydraulics.

Land Rover did not construct the Range Stormer itself, but entrusted the vehicle build to Stola in Turin, a company that specialized in prototype and concept-car construction. The full-size clay went out to Italy in August, while work was continuing on the interior design. This was led by Mark Butler, but also had considerable input from Ayline Koning,

ABOVE LEFT: **Sean Henstridge took the lead on exterior design of the Range Stormer.**

This 'teaser' picture was based on a rendering for the Range Stormer and was released to the press in September 2003 – before the real show car had been completed. The picture was shown to the assembled media during a presentation by Matthew Taylor at the Frankfurt Motor Show that month.

Another design rendering shows the interior concept. The strong centre console running back to the rear seat was not carried through to the production L320.

There were multiple 'concept car' features on the Range Stormer, together with several features that deliberately reflected the chosen design for the production L320.

who joined Land Rover in September 2003. It incorporated a 'sports command' driving position, similar in its effect to the one in the real L320, with a sweeping centre console and a high-set gear selector offset towards the driver.

The front seats were another deliberate piece of theatre, designed by Ayline Koning to look as if they were floating inside the cabin. They deliberately resembled a Möbius Strip (a surface with only one side and only one boundary), with the cushion and seat back flowing into the headrest in a continuous line. Built on an aluminium frame, they consisted of four layers of thick saddle leather laminated together on a thin GRP armature. Their edges were deliberately left raw and unfinished to resemble Scandinavian plywood furniture.

Stola had completed the Range Stormer by December 2003. The finished article had 22in alloy wheels – a size that was quite outrageous for the time – and was painted in a vivid candy-flake metallic colour that was given the name of Oh!Range. Also deliberately theatrical was a huge glass panoramic roof supported on four aluminium cross-braces, a concept that would eventually reach production Land Rover models on the Range Rover Evoque in 2011. The choice of the Range Stormer name was another masterstroke, retaining the link to the Range Rover brand but adding suggestions of dynamics and power.

The Range Stormer did everything that was required of it for the Detroit Show, and after spending some time in the entrance hall of Land Rover's Gaydon engineering centre, it was handed over to the British Motor Museum at Gaydon. Unfortunately, its dramatic doors no longer function: the

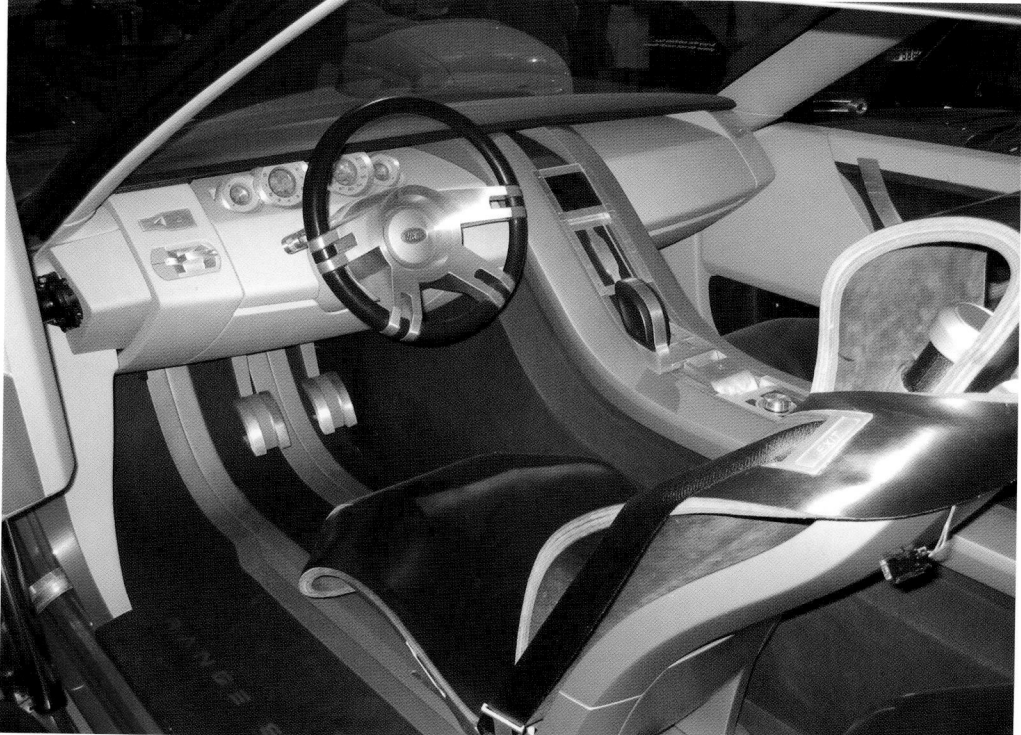

ABOVE LEFT: **The panoramic glass roof, heavily stylized exhaust outlets and rear window spoiler are all clear in this view.**

The interior design was considerably more radical than the exterior – although the exterior was radical in terms of Land Rover design.

Land Rover's MD introduces the Range Stormer at the January 2004 Detroit Motor Show. The theatrics with the doors were yet to come when this picture was taken.

hydraulic system was blown by a truck driver who was moving the vehicle, and as Stola had gone out of business by that stage, it has never been repaired.

If the Range Stormer was too obviously a theatrical show car for any thinking person to imagine that it foreshadowed the new model precisely, it certainly did its job of preparing the buying public for a change in Land Rover's orientation. So when the real Range Rover Sport was announced in January 2005, there was already eager anticipation among those in the market for such a vehicle.

The split-opening door design is clear in this picture taken at the British Motor Museum, where the Range Stormer now has a permanent home.
ALLEN WATKIN/WIKIMEDIA COMMONS

CHAPTER THREE

THE EARLY SPORT, 2005–2006

The first line-built Range Rover Sports were assembled in July 2004, and at this point the serial numbers changed from the 000500 sequence used for the hand-built prototypes to the 900000 series that would be used for production models. Nevertheless, it would be several months before production volumes were increased to create a pool of new vehicles for the showroom release in summer 2005. First, a large number of pilot-production models had to be built for validation testing, to prove assembly procedures, and for a variety of other purposes.

Land Rover's own records suggest that there were no fewer than 301 of these pilot-production models, and that the first 'full production' models were assembled in January 2005 to create that pool of vehicles for the Sales Division. The earliest of these was a diesel model with serial number 900302, and by extension all those with earlier numbers must be considered as pilot-production types.

In the meantime, the public relations and marketing teams had begun to prepare the ground for the new model's release. The first important date in their schedule was 25 November 2004, when UK media were sent a *First View* booklet, with photographs of pilot-production vehicles and an overview of the new model. In December, further details were released. The Range Rover Sport then made its world debut at the North American International Auto Show in Detroit on 10 January 2005, when Land Rover MD Matthew

Land Rover retained the first production Range Rover Sport. Registered BD55 YZZ, it was a left-hand-drive model with 19in V-spoke wheels and was painted Zermatt Silver.

Back at the Detroit Motor Show in January 2005, Matthew Taylor introduced the real thing – a Supercharged Sport in the First Edition colour of Vesuvius Orange.

Taylor was able to follow up on the 'tease' he had presented as the Range Stormer a year earlier.

The choice of a US motor show for the Sport's introduction was not merely a question of convenient timing. As customer research for the L320 programme had proceeded, it had quickly become apparent that the really big market for a sporty 4×4 vehicle was in the USA. The introduction of the Porsche Cayenne (a sporty SUV but without the Sport's off-road capability) to the USA in 2003 had simply served to confirm this, and so the Detroit Show was chosen as the ideal launch platform to gain publicity for the new model in the US market.

A few days later, on 19 January, prices and specifications for the UK market were released, confirming the new model's position in the Land Rover line-up between the Discovery 3 and the full-size Range Rover. Prices for the Discovery were mostly in the £30,000 segment; the Sport started at £34,995 and went on up to £58,995; and the 'full-size' Range Rover started at £45,995 and went on up to £60,995.

The next key date in the programme was April 2005, when the world-wide media launch event was held in Catalonia and journalists from around the world had their first chance to try the new model. This was a Land Rover event, of course, and so a large part of it was devoted to demonstrating that the Range Rover Sport had just as much off-road ability as any other Land Rover, in addition to its new-found on-road performance. The media came away suitably impressed.

The tailgate was a single-piece item with a window that could be opened separately for ease of access to the load area. This Java Black example appears from the exhaust tips and wheels to be a Supercharged model – but it was early enough not to have a Supercharged badge on the tailgate.

Land Rover's own view of its new model was neatly expressed in a quote attributed to Matthew Taylor and used in press material of the time. 'We see it as a less frenetic, more refined alternative to existing performance SUVs,' he said. 'Yet it is also exceptional off-road, offering better all-terrain ability than any competitor.' Back at Land Rover headquarters in Solihull, however, there was more excitement about the Sport than this somewhat matter-of-fact statement suggested. The indications were that the new model would appeal to a whole new group of customers and give Land Rover sales globally a significant boost. As things were to turn out, those indications were right on target.

A left-hand-drive Sport is put through some enjoyable off-road driving during the press launch event in Catalonia. The dark grey of the grille and side vents was known as Tungsten, and those are once again the 19in V-spoke wheels.

This kind of road showed the Sport at its best. The model is a left-hand-drive First Edition from the launch fleet.

VX54 EZK – AN EARLY SURVIVOR

Land Rover registered many of the pilot-production Sports with numbers that began VX54. The VX numbers were issued by the Worcester office of the DVLA, whose area included Solihull. A good number of these vehicles were left-hand-drive models that were intended for the press ride-and-drive in Catalonia, and when later sold on European markets they of course lost their distinctive British registration numbers.

One of those early 'VX54' cars had a most interesting history. VX54 EZK (SALLSAA345A-9000034) started life as a white left-hand-drive Supercharged model built to German specifications. However, the sales and marketing teams needed publicity pictures of a Supercharged model with the Vesuvius paint of the planned First Edition, and as no suitable example was available, VX54 EZK was repainted to fill in.

Bearing the dateless number plate EPS 402, it appeared in many early publicity pictures – which have sometimes caused confusion because the vehicle did not have the full First Edition specification. It did not have the 20in Stormer wheels, did not have a Supercharged badge on its tailgate, and did not have the standard Tungsten (grey) finish for the badge plinth at the bottom of its tailgate. This had been painted Vesuvius to match the bodywork when the colour had been changed!

After its publicity duties were over, VX54 EZK was sold to the Dunsfold Collection of Land Rovers, where it has since been re-registered as BA54 ALL to reflect the name of the collection's owner, Phil Bashall. It still has its original white paint in the engine bay, plus Rhodium interior contrast trim instead of the Lined Oak that was standard on First Edition models.

ABOVE LEFT: **When this early production model was repainted in Vesuvius Orange, the grey badge plinth at the rear was painted as well. As there was no Supercharged badge either, this rear view was a little confusing to anyone searching for the 'correct' specification!**

ABOVE RIGHT: **Truth will out: the original white paint is clearly visible on the inner wing of the publicity vehicle, which was not a First Edition model.**

THE 2005 AND 2006 MODELS

Showroom sales of the Range Rover Sport began in June 2005, with 2005 model-year vehicles that had been built in the previous six months to give dealers a launch stock. However, production of the 2005 models (identifiable by the 5A code in their VINs) lasted only over the summer. From approximately September, the Sports that left the assembly lines at Solihull were 2006 models (with a 6A identifying code). Not that they had any other significant differences: it was too early yet for Land Rover to make any changes to the specification on the basis of customer feedback. All they could do was adjust the production volumes of individual types and the colour and trim availability to match early indications of what would be popular.

Inevitably, the model line-up for 2005 and 2006 varied from one country to the next, but essentially there were three engines and four levels of trim and equipment. The engines were the 190bhp diesel that was expected to be the top seller in Europe and the UK, the mid-range 300bhp 4.4-litre petrol V8 that was largely intended for North America and the Middle East, and the range-topping 390bhp super-charged V8. Starting from the bottom, the specification levels were known as S, SE and HSE, the top level having no name of its own but being exclusive to the Supercharged models. On top of all this, there was an eye-catching First Edition Supercharged model that had deliberate visual links to the Range Stormer, and acted as a 'halo' product that helped to generate valuable showroom traffic.

Distinguishing one model from the next was not particularly easy unless the tailgate badging was visible. Entry-level S models had only a 'Sport' designator on the right of the panel; SE and HSE carried the appropriate letters below that badge; and the Supercharged models had a 'Supercharged' plaque directly below the Sport name. Supercharged models also had some special distinguishing features: a bright silver finish for the grille bars and side vents instead of the dull Tungsten finish standard on other models, twin stainless-steel exhaust tips, and unique Land Rover logos with silver lettering on black instead of gold on green.

The large and complex tail-lights can be seen here, and so can the HSE model identifier underneath the Sport badge. The grey plastic blob on the roof contained the antenna for the satellite navigation system.

RIGHT: **Full frontal: a left-hand-drive First Edition on forest tracks at the launch in Catalonia.**

Even though the Sport had been deliberately designed to have dynamic road behaviour, Land Rover had not neglected its off-road abilities. This Supercharged model with standard 20in wheels was pictured on the launch in Catalonia.

A distinctive silver-on-black Land Rover logo accompanied the silver-coloured grille bars on Supercharged models.

RIGHT: These 20in ten-spoke alloy wheels were specified for Supercharged models, when their centre caps also had black-on-silver logos.

The absence of rear identification theoretically would make this an early S model, but the 18in split-spoke alloy wheels seen here were only available with the SE specification.

The two-piece alloy wheels were a rare accessory. They are seen here on a Sport at the 2006 Geneva Show.
DRIVELINE CREATIVE MEDIA

The roof bars and roof box on a 2006 model from Land Rover's press fleet. This was actually a TDV6 with the HSE specification, although it also had the optional 20in ten-spoke alloy wheels.

Otherwise the wheel types and sizes were an aid to distinguishing one model from another. The entry-level S models had 17in wheels; there was an 18in size for the SE; HSE models had a 19in size; and the Supercharged models had 20in wheels. Of course, it was possible to order alternatives to the standard-fit wheels, and there was also a special 20in two-piece wheel available as a dealer-fit accessory, and so the wheels were not a wholly reliable way of identifying a Range Rover Sport.

THE TECHNOLOGY

The new Range Rover Sport was unquestionably the most technologically advanced Land Rover yet built, and press officers were more than happy to get that message across to journalists whenever they could. They were less happy to engage in dialogue about why the 'full-size' Range Rover did not have some of that new technology, although they would of course have known that Terrain Response and six-speed gearboxes were in the planning stages for introduction a year or so later.

A great deal of the new technology was devoted to giving the new Sport a dynamic on-road behaviour that was worthy of its name. Active roll mitigation was standard on all models. So were ETC (electronic traction control), EBA (electronic brake assist, which applied full braking power automatically if it sensed an emergency) and DSC (dynamic stability control). DSC monitored wheel speed and steering angle to give safer and more stable cornering, and could apply individual wheel brakes to correct over-steer or under-steer and keep the vehicle under control. The Dynamic Response system was standard only on the Supercharged models, sensing cornering forces and compensating for them to give crisper handling; it also decoupled the anti-roll bars when low range was selected in the transfer box to give more wheel articulation for off-road driving.

Then there were E-diffs (electronic differentials) front and rear, which depended on signals from the steering system and the engine to control the power directed to each wheel so that all wheels were supplied with the torque they needed. An active locking rear differential was on the options list, but realistically was not likely to be needed on any model except the Supercharged ones.

The Sport also became the first Land Rover ever to have adaptive cruise control (ACC), and those models that had this option carried a distinctive black plastic plate in the front bumper aperture with the letters ACC. ACC was linked to the standard cruise control system, and worked by using a radar beam to detect the vehicle ahead. It could be set to maintain a chosen distance from that vehicle automatically, and like ordinary cruise control, could be over-ridden by the brake or accelerator pedal.

Topping off the technology on these first models was an optional (and formidably expensive) Bi-Xenon adaptive front lighting system. Not only did it depend on Xenon lighting technology, which delivered a particularly intense light, but it could also vary the amount of light that the headlights cast on to the road to suit the speed and direction of the vehicle. The headlights themselves could move from side to side or up and down to make these variations, and they could follow the curve of the road in exactly the same way as a driver's eyes.

This discreet black plastic panel betrayed the presence of the automatic cruise control option.

In mid-2005 much of this sounded like technology for technology's sake – but Land Rover knew what they were doing. Their aim was to create a strong image of high technology around the Range Rover Sport to help give it a distinctive place in the Land Rover model line-up. It was a ploy that proved very successful indeed, and paved the way for the acceptance of high technology features on other Land Rover models later on.

INTERIOR DESIGN

There was no shortage of technology inside the passenger cabin. Every Range Rover Sport came with a dual-zone automatic air-conditioning system that incorporated a particulates filter. For safety, there were altogether eight airbags, including a side curtain bag over each door. Standard, too, was a touchscreen-operated satellite navigation system that worked both on and off the road, and an option was a Nokia voice recognition system for the navigation and audio controls. There was a Bluetooth link to suit mobile phones, too.

There was also an impressive array of in-car entertainment systems. A high quality harmon/kardon audio system was standard on every model, and right at the top of the hierarchy was that company's LOGIC 7 system that featured fourteen speakers and a twelve-channel digitally controlled amplifier with 50 watts per channel to create a 'surround sound' stage in the cabin. Key among these speakers were a centre-fill unit in the dashboard and a 28cm (11in) subwoofer mounted in the tailgate. The LOGIC 7 head unit was integrated within the facia, and was capable of storing six CDs. Being able to play MP3 files on CDs as well gave what Land Rover described as a sixty-six album music capacity – once again a case of technology being used to impress.

For rear-seat passengers there was also the option of a twin-screen DVD system, with a 16.5cm (6.5in) video screen embedded in the rear face of each front-seat headrest. This system was completed by a six-DVD changer mounted in the loadspace.

Beside all this, the question of the interior colour and trim sounds almost unimportant, but the choices did allow considerable variations in the interior ambience, from deliberately sporty to unashamedly luxurious. There was fabric upholstery for the entry-level S models, but all others had leather: plain leather for the SE models, ruched ('Premium') leather for the HSE, and a special Sports leather for the Supercharged variants, with perforations and a bright silver backing that could be seen through those perforations.

The high centre console enhanced the 'cockpit' feel of the driving position, which is seen here on a Supercharged model with perforated leather upholstery and standard Rhodium contrast trim.

With light-coloured Alpaca upholstery and Cherry Wood contrast trim a completely different interior ambience was created.

This rear seat is upholstered in standard leather, with neither ruches nor perforations. The three head restraints were all adjustable for height, and the seat had a one-third/two-thirds split folding ability to increase the load space.

Rear-seat passengers had their own adjustable air-distribution vents in the back of the cubby box.

The electronic handbrake ('parking brake' to Land Rover) was operated by the paddle switch nearest the camera. Behind is the rotary control for the Terrain Response system, while the yellow switch engages Hill Descent Control and the other two adjust the suspension height and select low range in the transfer box.

Four upholstery colours were available, and there were multiple possibilities by combining these with contrast trim panels. Mounted on the dashboard and door cards, these were the modern equivalent of wood trim, and indeed there was a Cherry Wood option, which had the effect of giving the interior a luxurious feel. However, the standard contrast trim was Rhodium, a grey plastic that gave a deliberately 'technical' feel to the passenger cabin and was entirely in keeping with the Sport's sporting pre-tensions.

THE FIRST EDITION

The First Edition Supercharged model was planned to give the Sport a high profile from the moment the new model reached showrooms. Its orange paint – called Vesuvius – was not the same as the Oh!Range on the Range Stormer show car, but was deliberately similar to it and was not available on any other model. It was also impossible to miss when the First Edition was out on the streets. In theory, the Vesuvius paint was an option, but it seems likely that few First Edition models were ordered without it.

Special wheels, appropriately known as the Stormer design, were also a deliberate reflection of those on the show car, although their diameter was a mere 20in instead of the 22in on the Range Stormer. Like all Supercharged models, the First Edition had a Sports leather interior, but in this case the contrast panels were in Lined Oak, which was not available elsewhere (at this stage) and gave an interest-ing balance between luxury and sportiness. Land Rover went to some pains to point out that the Lined Oak was hand-polished, but unfortunately this led to all sorts of misnomers in sales and service literature, such as Hand Lined Oak and even Hand Limed Oak. Bright tread strips and Range Rover Sport branded overmats added further special touches.

The overall quantities of the First Edition are not known, but there were just 150 of these special models for the UK,

This press launch picture was quite widely used but is actually misleading. The wheels belong to a standard Supercharged model, but the Vesuvius Orange paint was exclusive to the First Edition, which had different wheels.

a figure that helped to justify their high cost and made them very exclusive machines.

ACCESSORIES

Land Rover had learned a valuable lesson with the first Discovery model back in 1989: that a large range of accessories sells well because it allows customers to personalize their vehicles. As the Range Rover Sport was very much a vehicle that customers were going to buy for its individual qualities, the company prepared a large range of accessories to go with it.

Accessories, by definition, were available through Land Rover dealers but could not normally be fitted on the assembly lines. Aftermarket companies soon began to produce cheaper alternatives to some of them, but the typical first owner of a Range Rover Sport tended to go for the genuine factory accessory, which was very often branded with the Land Rover logo.

The accessories available in the early days of the Range Rover Sport are described below.

Wheels and Associated Items

A 20in two-piece five-spoke alloy wheel was available as an accessory fit (note that the V-spoke 19in, ten-spoke 20in and Stormer 20in could all be fitted as line options if they were not already standard on the model). Front and rear mudflaps were available, as were snow chains for the front wheels (only) when 18in and 19in wheels were specified. There was no snow chain option for the 20in wheels.

Exterior Fittings

For protection, there were rubber body side mouldings and a front A-frame (made of black impact-resistant plastic). There were also plastic-coated metal guards for headlamps and tail-lights. A driving- and fog-lamp assembly was available, to fit on the A-frame.

To aid access, there were side steps that fitted below the doors but remained visible as a bright metal strip when the doors were closed. For cosmetic enhancement, it was also possible to buy a chromed top section for the door mirror bodies.

Carrying Equipment

There were multiple options for carrying things on the roof, and central to all of them was a set of roof rails that locked into special receivers. Adding a set of crossbars to these created a conventional roofrack. A luggage box or (smaller) sports-equipment box could be added, as could a ski and snowboard carrier or an aqua sports-equipment carrier. A luggage carrier could also be fitted, and there were optional ratchet straps to secure items to the roof carrier.

A bicycle carrier was also available, but had to be secured to a towbar.

Towing Equipment

Towing equipment varied to some extent from country to country to meet local regulations. In Britain, the options were a multi-height (adjustable) towbar or a quick-release (swan-neck) towbar, in each case with towing electrics. An option was an electrical socket suitable for powering camping equipment.

Interior Enhancements

There were both cosmetic and functional accessory options for the interior. The cosmetic ones were carpet overmats in Alpaca, Aspen or Ebony (although Alpaca was soon deleted), rubber footwell mats, and sill tread plates. A contrast trim-panel kit in Cherry Wood or Lined Oak was available for customers who regretted taking the standard-fit Rhodium trim!

Functional interior accessories were waterproof seat covers for both the front and rear seats, a hands-free phone system, and an add-on rear-seat entertainment system (a system with headrest-mounted screens was a line-build option). This consisted of a foldaway 43cm (16.9in) DVD screen and DVD player, both mounted under the roof, and headphones were available as an extra-cost option.

There were load-space options, too. A metal mesh cargo barrier doubled as a dog guard and came with a useful 'ski hatch' so that long loads could still be carried when it was in place. A divider of the same construction could be ordered to split the load space into two – again, suitable if two dogs were being carried and needed to be kept apart. A rubber load-space mat and a rigid load-space protector could be had, plus a waterproof load-space liner. A load retention net with two ratchet straps was a further option, and there was even a sliding load-space floor, which made access to the far end of the load space considerably easier for short people.

WHAT THE PRESS THOUGHT

Understandably it was the flagship Supercharged model that attracted the most enthusiastic press reviews, even though the bestseller was always going to be the TDV6. Nevertheless the Automobile Association's magazine *Motoring* seemed dead set against it in its April 2005 issue. The review read:

> If you object to urban SUVs on principle, [the Sport] embodies everything you dislike in one package. As an in-your-face example of urban consumerism, it's in a league of its own. [It is also] far from family friendly. Rear seats feel like a bit of an afterthought, lacking trays, extensive storage areas and other features required by kids.

Acknowledging its excellent off-road ability, but also questioning the practical value of that ability, the review concluded that:

> On-road it's impressive, able to mix it with sports cars in the outside lane and show them a clean pair of heels – provided you can cope with hideous fuel consumption and emissions figures......Acceleration and braking are worthy of a sports car, but it's hard not to question the wisdom of driving a vehicle of this size in the manner of a roadster.

By contrast, a drive in the Supercharged model at the press launch in Spain left Simon Hodder of *Land Rover Enthusiast* magazine very impressed. In the June 2005 issue he wrote:

> The Sport has something that has been lacking in LRs of late – a soul. A vehicle either has character or it doesn't, and this one's got it by the bucket load.... it just begs you to drive it enthusiastically, and of course, it would be rude not to, would it not?.... I challenge anyone to sit in the driver's seat and not get the urge to see just what 390bhp really feels like.

The road performance was wholly convincing: 'Steering is more precise than you'd think possible in a Land Rover, and the brakes, particularly on the Supercharged models, are simply superb.' And yet the new model had lost none of the traditional Land Rover off-road capabilities: 'Land Rover threw it at one of the most serious rock climbs I've ever seen a standard vehicle attempt, and it succeeded admirably.'

Child Safety

There were three add-on child seat options. One was a baby seat secured by the rear seatbelt; one was an ISOFIX child seat, secured by ISO standard fittings; and the third was a child booster seat. All of these were proprietary items that could be supplied through Land Rover dealers.

Extras

Finally there was a miscellaneous group of items that Range Rover Sport owners might find useful. These were not exclusive to the model but were promoted in accessory catalogues for the Sport. They consisted of a foot pump, a first-aid kit, a fire extinguisher, a spare bulb kit, a warning triangle, a tow strap, an electric coolbag and – for lovers of the outdoor life – a day tent that could be supplied at extra cost with a connection tunnel to attach it to the vehicle.

CUSTOMERS AND COLOURS

It soon became apparent that the Range Rover Sport had found a new group of enthusiastic customers for Land Rover. For the most part, these were not at all like traditional Land Rover customers: the off-road capability of the vehicle was very much incidental to the purchase, and the 4×4 drivetrain was seen mostly as providing traction benefits on the road in wet or snowy conditions. These customers were necessarily

---

There was one major drawback to the flagship Supercharged models, though, and that was fuel consumption. 'You should be able to get about 17mpg,' thought Simon, 'but drive it in a spirited manner, and you won't find it too difficult to get it down into single figures, if you want to.'

The TDV6 diesels met with mixed reviews. *Top Gear* magazine for November 2005 reported that:

It's not bad to drive, but let's not get carried away. The steering is remote, but accurate when you get used to it. The suspension does a great job of keeping it all going in the same direction and on the same piece of road that you suggest via the wheel.

In this 'most reasonable of all the versions', fuel consumption was quite good at 8ltr/100km (35.4mpg), and 'the ride comfort is noticeably better on the 19in wheels than the 20s on the Supercharged car.'

The Independent newspaper wondered, in its issue of 10 January 2006:

…whether the diesel model tested here really deserves the appellation 'Sport', which fits the much speedier petrol versions rather better. But the diesel is so sweet and tractable that you'd have to be unreasonably mean to grumble about that.

A selection of readers invited to give their opinions reported that:

…as a motorway tool it is excellent, with a good view of the road ahead, low noise levels and a great cabin… Off-road it is simply staggering – and very accessible to the novice… The turbodiesel V6 performed well considering the weight it has to pull around, even if it was a bit sluggish on acceleration.

Respected weekly magazine *Autocar*, however, was not very enthusiastic. Of the TDV6 model, it wrote in its issue dated 16 February 2006 that:

…even with a brilliant diesel engine it lacks the pizzazz and charm of the petrol models. With sluggish off-the-line performance you question the Sport moniker as well, even though it is remarkably agile for its size and weight.

well off or even wealthy: they wanted and could afford a luxurious vehicle that was expensive to run, but they also wanted a very individualized vehicle that did not have the rather grand associations of the full-size Range Rover.

Brasher and more glamorous than the full-size Range Rover, the Sport was soon adopted by celebrities and others who expected to be noticed. In its early years it attracted a clientèle whom full-size Range Rover buyers sometimes characterized as *nouveau riche*, and whom many onlookers in Britain characterized – or caricatured – as Premier League footballers. The Supercharged model with its stupendous performance (and cost) was tailored precisely for such people, and the lesser models bathed in its reflected glory.

There were inevitably some people within Land Rover itself who regretted this change of target customer, but they could not argue against the business case that it made for the company. The Range Rover Sport was the single product that helped Land Rover reorient itself towards a fashionable clientèle, allowing prices and profits to increase, and fundamentally changing public perceptions of what the Land Rover name represented.

Car buyers in Britain during the mid-2000s had entered on a period of caution when it came to colour choice. Blacks, silvers, greys and dark blues were in favour, supposedly on the grounds that they were readily acceptable and made a car easier to sell on when the time came. As a result, these were the colours that predominated on the Range Rover Sport, despite the best efforts of the Land Rover designers to provide a range of attractive options.

COLOUR AND TRIM OPTIONS, 2005–2006 MODELS

There were twelve paint options when the Sport was introduced in 2005, of which one was confined to the First Edition Supercharged models. Maya Gold was dropped for the 2006 model-year and Vesuvius Orange had also gone, leaving ten options. All these paints were metallic types except for Chawton White, which was a traditional 'solid' type.

In specifying a new Range Rover Sport, customers could also choose from four upholstery colours and two contrast panel options (plus a third that was exclusive to the First Edition). Most combinations were feasible, although Land Rover did refuse to provide some combinations that they considered did not work; in sales catalogues they also highlighted the ones they thought worked best by describing them as 'designer's choice' options.

Premium leather was softer than standard leather and was ruched. Sports leather had perforations, through which a bright metallic backing was visible.

COLOUR OPTIONS

Paint	Codes	Notes
Arctic Frost	962, MBH	Designer's choice with Aspen upholstery and Cherry Wood trim
Bonatti Grey	659, LAL	
Buckingham Blue	796, JGJ	
Cairns Blue	849, JEU	Not available with Aspen upholstery
Chawton White	603, NAL	
Giverny Green	734, HZB	Designer's choice with Aspen or Ivory upholstery
Java Black	697, PNF	
Maya Gold	846, GAN	Designer's choice with Alpaca upholstery and Cherry Wood trim Not available with Ivory upholstery Available only until October 2005
Rimini Red	889, CBK	Not available with Aspen or Ivory upholstery
Tonga Green	904, HFY	Designer's choice with Ivory upholstery and Cherry Wood trim
Vesuvius Orange	811, EYS	Only available on First Edition Supercharged models Sports leather upholstery and hand-polished Lined Oak trim standard
Zambezi Silver	737, MVC	

UPHOLSTERY OPTIONS

Specification	Material	Colour options
S	Fabric	Alpaca, Ebony
SE	Leather (fabric optional at no cost)	Alpaca, Aspen, Ebony
HSE	Premium leather	Alpaca, Ebony, Ivory
Supercharged	Sports leather	Ebony, Ivory

Carpets and Main Interior Trim Panels

The combinations were dependent on the upholstery colour, and were as follows:

With Alpaca upholstery: Ebony carpets with Ebony or Ivory panels

With Aspen upholstery: Aspen carpets and panels on SE
Aspen carpets and Ivory panels on HSE

With Ebony upholstery: Ebony carpets and panels

With Ivory upholstery: Aspen carpets with Aspen or Ivory panels
Ebony carpets with Ebony or Ivory panels

Contrast Panel Options

The standard contrast panels were Rhodium, but Cherry Wood was optional at no extra cost. The First Edition, uniquely, came with hand-polished Lined Oak panels.

WHEEL AND TYRE OPTIONS, 2005 AND 2006 MODEL-YEARS

Specification	
S	17in with five split spokes and 235/65R17 tyres
	Optional 18in with ten spokes and 255/55R18 tyres
SE	18in with five split spokes and 255/55R18 tyres
	Optional 19in with five V-spokes and 255/50R19 tyres (as SE)
HSE	19in with five V-spokes and 255/50R19 tyres
Supercharged	20in with ten spokes and 275/40R20 tyres
First Edition	20in Stormer with nine spokes and 275/40R20 tyres

17 INCH, 5 SPLIT SPOKE ALLOYS   18 INCH, 10 SPOKE ALLOYS

18 INCH, 5 SPLIT SPOKE ALLOYS   19 INCH, 5V SPOKE ALLOYS

20 INCH, 10 SPOKE ALLOYS   20 INCH, 'STORMER' ALLOYS*

The six wheel options available at the start of Range Rover Sport production.

SPECIAL EDITIONS

The HST Model

Aiming to give sales of the Sport a boost over the summer of 2006 before the new 2007 models arrived in the autumn, Land Rover produced another special-edition model based on the Supercharged specification. The Range Rover Sport Supercharged HST (normally known simply as the HST) was announced at the Goodwood Festival of Speed in June, and sales began more or less immediately.

This first HST (there would be another one later) was a 2006 model-year vehicle, even though sales continued into the start of the 2007 model-year. It became the new top model in the Sport range for 2007 in Britain, with a price of £63,000 that put it well into full-size Range Rover territory and made it the most expensive Sport derivative yet. It was, said official literature, 'Range Rover Sport's ultimate expression of power and status'. The key feature of the HST was a bodykit that consisted of angular front and rear aprons, a larger tail spoiler, and rectangular tail-pipes. This kit was in turn supposedly inspired by the Range Stormer concept, and it was accompanied by a very full specification.

Land Rover never did explain what the HST designation stood for, but few buyers probably cared. Just five exterior colours were offered: Bonatti Grey, Cairns Blue, Java Black, Rimini Red and Zermatt Silver. The new model came with 20in Stormer alloy wheels and chromed aluminium side-

The HST also came with twin rectangular exhaust outlets. The correct production Supercharged tailgate badge is also in evidence here.

vents, body-colour lower doors and tailgate badge plinth, rear privacy glass (which could be deleted), and an electric sunroof and automatic cruise control as standard. A rear e-differential was standard. Upholstery was the standard Supercharged fare of Ebony or Ivory Sports leather, in either case with Ebony carpets, and the standard contrast trim was Lined Oak.

There were those at Land Rover who freely admitted that they did not like the HST bodykit at all, but there was no doubt that the company had correctly anticipated the way the market would go for the Range Rover Sport. Within the next few months, a number of aftermarket specialists would bring their own bodykits to market to meet a growing demand for a Sport that looked different.

The angular lines of the bodykit designed for the HST model were very much a matter of taste – but they were more tasteful than some of the aftermarket offerings that followed.

The Piet Boon Edition

Dutch architect and designer Piet Boon had developed a long-term relationship with Land Rover in the Netherlands, and designed a number of special-edition models for them as a result. In May 2006, the Piet Boon design edition Range Rover Sport was announced, a fifteen-strong special edition based on the Supercharged Sport. It cost €15,000 on top of the price for a standard Supercharged model, which in the Netherlands at that time stood at €108,200.

The key exterior features were Dark Grey High Solid paint, angular exhaust outlets, and roof bars finished in brushed stainless steel. There was a 'PB Edition' badge on

A solid paint finish and roof bars in contrasting brushed stainless steel marked out the 2006 Piet Boon edition.

The Range Rover plinth at the bottom of the tailgate was painted in the body colour, and there were Piet Boon identifying badges.

Contemporary design: the exhaust tips had a hewn-from-solid look to them.

the tailgate. The seats were re-upholstered with Piet Boon's own leather, and some interior details were painted black or given a special stainless-steel or alloy appearance. In addition, each example came with an exclusive Piet Boon set of luggage.

LAND ROVER IN 2006

The year 2006 was a busy one for Land Rover, and the success of the Range Rover Sport is best understood against that background. This was a year when the company began in earnest to address environmental concerns associated with its vehicles; and it was a year when it was heavily committed to the second G4 Challenge adventure sports event that promoted its vehicles on a global stage.

Environmental Matters

The early 2000s saw a rise in public concerns about environmental damage caused by human activity, and among the activities singled out as particularly damaging was the use of cars. CO_2 emissions had been identified as a major cause of global warming, and (beginning in the USA) activists focused on the CO_2 emissions in vehicle exhausts – especially in the exhausts of those with large engines.

Inevitably this made Land Rover a target of environmental activists as well. In May 2005, thirty-five protesters identifying with the environmental protection group Greenpeace invaded the Solihull factory and brought production to a halt. Sneaking past security as shifts changed at 7am, they chained themselves to part-built vehicles. After more than a dozen had been arrested for trespass, the remaining protesters left peacefully in mid-afternoon, but not before they had prevented an estimated £3.8 million worth of cars being built.

Land Rover subsequently claimed that they were already working on plans to reduce their environmental footprint, and that they had shown these to Greenpeace representatives before the protest, but clearly to no avail. One way or another, those plans became public knowledge during 2006.

The plans had two dimensions. On the one hand, Land Rover was working on a suite of new technologies for future vehicles that would reduce their environmental impact. However, the company was well aware that no amount of investment could speed up development of these new technologies to match the perceived urgency of the problem. So

LAND ROVER

RECALL NOTICE

TO OWNERS OF DISCOVERIES AND RANGE ROVERS

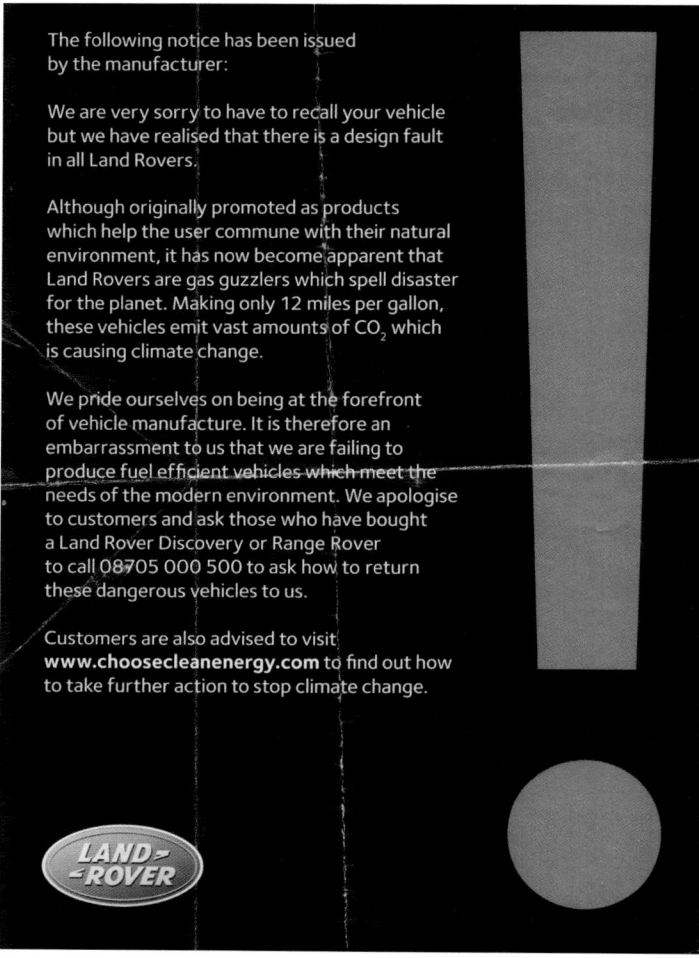

The following notice has been issued by the manufacturer:

We are very sorry to have to recall your vehicle but we have realised that there is a design fault in all Land Rovers.

Although originally promoted as products which help the user commune with their natural environment, it has now become apparent that Land Rovers are gas guzzlers which spell disaster for the planet. Making only 12 miles per gallon, these vehicles emit vast amounts of CO_2 which is causing climate change.

We pride ourselves on being at the forefront of vehicle manufacture. It is therefore an embarrassment to us that we are failing to produce fuel efficient vehicles which meet the needs of the modern environment. We apologise to customers and ask those who have bought a Land Rover Discovery or Range Rover to call 08705 000 500 to ask how to return these dangerous vehicles to us.

Customers are also advised to visit **www.choosecleanenergy.com** to find out how to take further action to stop climate change.

ABOVE LEFT AND RIGHT: **In 2005–2006, Land Rover had to contend with trouble from environmental protesters. This flyer was left on the windscreens of vehicles that offended the sensibilities of activists.**

Sports were used as crew vehicles on the 2006 G4 Challenge; this one was crewed by Gabriel Maldonado from Spain and Claribett Vega from the combined Chilean and Costa Rican teams.

Technical Specifications, 2005–2006

Engines
(1) TDV6 2.7-litre diesel
2720cc (81 × 88mm) Ford-Peugeot ohv V6 diesel with 4
  valves per cylinder, common-rail injection, turbocharger and
  intercooler (early versions EU3 compliant; EU4 versions
  from January 2007)
Siemens PDC2 engine-management system
18:1 compression ratio
190bhp at 4,000rpm
325lb/ft at 1,900rpm

(2) 4.4-litre Jaguar V8 petrol
4394cc (88 × 90.3mm) Jaguar AJ-8 petrol V8 with four
  camshafts and 4 valves per cylinder
Denso EMS generation 1 engine-management system
10.75:1 compression ratio
300bhp at 5,500rpm
315lb/ft at 4,000rpm

(3) 4.2-litre Supercharged V8 petrol
4197cc (86 × 90.3mm) Jaguar AJ-8 petrol V8 with four
  camshafts and 4 valves per cylinder, plus Eaton supercharger
  and intercooler
Denso EMS generation 1 engine-management system
9.1:1 compression ratio
390bhp at 5,750rpm
410lb/ft at 3,500rpm

Transmission
Permanent four-wheel drive with centre differential
  incorporating viscous coupling to give automatic locking;
  Terrain Response traction system standard; optional locking
  rear differential

Final drive ratio: 3.73:1 (V8 petrol models)
           3.54:1 (TDV6 and V8 supercharged models)

Primary gearbox:
Six-speed ZF 6HP26 automatic; ratios 4.171:1, 2.340:1,
  1.521:1, 1.143:1, 0.867:1, 0.691:1, reverse 3.403:1

Transfer gearbox:
Separate two-speed type with 'active' centre differential; high
  ratio 1:1, low ratio 2.93:1

Suspension
Independent front and rear suspension with height-adjustable
  electronic air suspension and telescopic dampers; double
  wishbones front and rear

Steering
ZF Servotronic speed proportional power-assisted rack and
  pinion

Brakes
Four-wheel disc brakes with dual hydraulic line, servo
  assistance and Bosch four-channel ABS
Ventilated front discs with 317mm diameter (TDV6), 337mm
  diameter (4.4 V8) or 360mm diameter (supercharged V8),
  with four-piston callipers
Ventilated rear discs with 325mm diameter single-piston
  callipers (TDV6 and V8 models), or 350mm diameter and
  four-piston callipers (supercharged V8 and TDV8)
Servo-operated parking brake operating on drums within the
  rear discs

Vehicle dimensions

Wheelbase:	2,745mm (108.1in)
Overall length:	4,788mm (188.5in)
Overall width:	1,928mm (75.9in); 2,170mm (85.4in) over mirrors
Overall height:	1,817mm (71.5in) at standard ride height
Unladen weight	(1) 2.7-litre diesel models: 2,455kg (5,412lb)
(for typical	(2) 4.4-litre petrol models: 2,480kg (5,468lb)
UK-market	(3) 4.2-litre supercharged V8 models: 2,572kg
models):	(5,670lb)

Performance
(1) 2.7-litre TDV6 models

Max. speed:	193km/h (120mph)
0–60mph:	11.9sec

(2) 4.4-litre petrol V8 models

Max. speed:	209km/h (130mph)
0–60mph:	8.2sec

(3) 4.2-litre V8 Supercharged models

Max. speed:	225km/h (140mph)
0–60mph:	7.2sec

in parallel with developing these new technologies, it took steps to mitigate the immediate impact by introducing a CO_2 Offset scheme from the start of the 2007 model-year in the autumn.

The new technologies became public knowledge at the Geneva Show in March 2006, when Land Rover displayed the rather awkwardly named Land_e. This was a Freelander-sized skeleton model that presented fuel-saving ideas, and ideas for lightweight, hybrid electric and bio-fuel vehicles. Most of these technologies were a long way in the future, but the Land_e did at least demonstrate that Land Rover had made a start.

The CO_2 Offset Programme was then announced to the media on 18 July. Scheduled to run until 2008 and to act as a pilot scheme, this was run in conjunction with Climate Care Ltd. There were two parts to it, one offsetting emissions generated by vehicle assembly at the Solihull and Halewood factories, and the other being a levy charged on top of the showroom price of each vehicle that 'bought' 72,400km (45,000 miles) worth of offset. While the vehicles continued to produce undesirable amounts of CO_2, the levy was paid directly into aid schemes around the world that made an immediate reduction in locally produced quantities of CO_2.

The idea was a little creaky, but it did buy Land Rover time while they developed the promised new technologies. Owner Ford supported the initiative by announcing in July that it planned to spend at least £1 billion developing a range of global environmental technologies in the UK for its Ford, Jaguar, Land Rover and Volvo brands.

The G4 Challenge

After Land Rover had pulled out of the Camel Trophy international adventure challenge event in 1998, the com-

pany's Marketing Department began to make plans for a replacement. This materialized in 2003 as the G4 Challenge – the G4 referred to four geographical zones where stages would take place – and the idea was to focus more on challenges to the individual than on the team spirit of the Camel Trophy. The first event was planned to showcase all four Land Rover product ranges – Defender, Freelander, Discovery and Range Rover – and a fleet of vehicles was specially prepared, using an eye-catching Tangiers Orange colour scheme.

A second G4 Challenge was held in 2006, and as before, featured examples of all Land Rover's current range of vehicles. This time there were five of them, as the Range Rover Sport had been added to the line-up. The nature of the event also changed slightly, because the 2003 event had been widely criticized as having insufficient focus on the vehicles and too much on the adventure-sports element.

A total of thirty-five 4.4-litre HSE Sports with right-hand drive were prepared for the event, one becoming a publicity vehicle. One vehicle put in a token appearance in Brazil for that leg of the event; thirteen more were used by the press on the Bolivian leg; and the remaining twenty were used by competitors and support staff during the stages of the event held in Thailand. The vehicles were equipped with a number of items from the accessories list, together with a special roofrack (by Monacar), a Warn winch, and a Mantec sump guard and raised air intake. They were all painted in Tangiers Orange, and wore G4 Challenge decals and other identification.

These vehicles were mostly sold off in Britain after the event was over. Some have since been reregistered, and some have allegedly even been repainted for buyers who did not want the Tangiers Orange paint. However, genuine survivors can be recognized by that paint, and by number plates in three sequences, beginning BL05, BN55 and BV55.

CHAPTER FOUR

NEW IDEAS, NEW CHALLENGES, 2007–2009

With the L320 Sport firmly established in global markets during its first two years on sale, Land Rover were able to anticipate strong sales during 2007, and the model did not disappoint. But any elation associated with that was short-lived, because sales were badly hit by a global recession in mid-2008.

The 2007 calendar year was an exceptionally good one for Land Rover's global sales, and in December the company announced that it had exceeded 200,000 sales in a year for the first time ever. The Range Rover Sport had made an important contribution to that figure, with a production total of nearly 62,000 vehicles. However, it was also in December 2007 that the early signs of a major global economic decline became apparent. The next two years would be a roller-coaster ride for Land Rover as a whole, and inevitably the Range Rover Sport was affected.

The 2007 calendar-year production total would be the highest that the Sport ever achieved. By the middle of 2008, the effects of that economic decline (generally now described as a recession) had become only too clear, and

The Sport was soon considered sufficiently glamorous to be worth the cost of special number plates like this one, issued in 2007.

MICHAEL HARNETT

sales of all Land Rover models went into free-fall. Production at the Solihull and Halewood factories was adjusted to suit, and by late August Land Rover was cutting production shifts and had transferred nearly 300 staff from Solihull to the Jaguar plant at Castle Bromwich because there was no work for them on the Land Rover lines. Range Rover Sport production for the 2008 calendar year ended up 25 per cent down on 2007. The following year was even worse, with a further 36 per cent drop in production; the 2009 calendar year figures for the Sport were less than 50 per cent of those for 2007. And yet the Sport, perhaps one of the most unlikely vehicles to bounce back after such a traumatic period, survived.

THE 2007 MODELS AND THE TDV8

A late start to the 2007 model-year gave dealers time to move stocks of the summer-special HST model before the new season's models were introduced. Their announcement had been held back to allow the full-size Range Rover to be first into the market with a new diesel engine option, but it was only a matter of weeks before the TDV8 engine was announced as a fourth engine option for the Sport as well. It was accompanied by some minor revisions to the Sport's

specification, changes to the paint and trim options, and some new accessories.

The TDV8 Engine

The new TDV8 was a 3.6-litre, 4-valve diesel V8 with twin turbochargers, built specifically for the Range Rover and Range Rover Sport, and designed to give Land Rover a high-performance diesel in Europe, where V8 diesels were beginning to appear in SUV models from other manufacturers. With 268bhp and simply massive torque of 472lb/ft at 2,000rpm – far more than the supercharged petrol V8 – it was a quite remarkable engine.

Its origins lay in the 1998 Gemini agreement between Ford and Peugeot-Citroën to develop a new family of diesel engines for joint use. At that stage Land Rover had still belonged to BMW, but after the Ford takeover in 2000 the company had access to the 2.7-litre diesel V6 that was part of the programme, and eagerly adapted it for their own use as the TDV6.

Ford were keen to replace the BMW diesel engine in the full-size Range Rover as soon as possible, and initially considered the twin-turbocharged Jaguar version of the diesel V6 to maintain a distinction from the single-turbo version planned for L319 and L320. However, it soon became clear

The TDV8 diesel engine took centre stage among the 2007 model-year introductions.

that there were installation problems in the L322 Range Rover, and that the only solution was to create a new diesel engine.

Ever since the start of the Gemini programme, Ford had kept in mind the possibility of developing a V8 version of the new large-capacity diesel, but Peugeot-Citroën had no interest in such an engine and so it did not become part of the joint programme. However, Ford were free to draw on the Gemini technology as they saw fit, and by early 2001 they were envisaging a V8 diesel as ideal for both the Range Rover and the forthcoming Range Rover Sport. From early on, they called it the Lion V8, just as the V6 diesel had been known as the Lion V6, in honour of Peugeot's lion logo.

At this stage, Ford saw the engine as very much their own project, even though it was being drawn up for Range Rovers. Outline planning began during March that year at the Ford research centre in Aachen, Germany, and at Land Rover, Grant Horne was appointed as manager for the new engine programme. He remembered some years later:

As you might expect, the Ford people did look at other potential applications. Jaguar XJ and XK were among them, but they decided not to go ahead with them. That made our life easier because we were designing for just one application and didn't have to take into account requirements for other applications!

Although there were several common elements between the V6 and V8 diesel designs, there were also many differences. 'Ultimate refinement was one of the drivers in the Range Rover programme', according to Grant, and so the 60-degree angle of the V6 block was changed for the 90-degree angle that gives smoother running with a V8 configuration. This in turn created some extra challenges associated with the oil drain for the twin turbochargers, which were to be mounted low down for packaging reasons. So to guarantee satisfactory performance at the extreme operating angles associated with off-road use, the designers chose a scavenge pump.

Packaging was again behind the decision to mount the V8's injection pump at the front of the engine rather than at the rear, but the choice of a chain drive instead of the V6's belt drive was prompted by expectations of greater stresses in the larger engine. The combustion chamber design – the most expensive and time-consuming element in designing a modern diesel engine – was carried over directly from the V6, and as a result the bore and stroke dimensions of the two engines were the same. This commonality was also expected to allow for both V6 and V8 diesel engines to be assembled on the same lines at Ford's Dagenham diesel engines plant in Britain. As on the V6, the cylinder block of the V8 was to be made from compacted graphite iron, with the minimum metal around the bores and below the crank centre-line.

By early 2003 the design had been completed, and Ford handed the diesel V8 over to Land Rover as a CAD package. Development now began, with Land Rover engineers joining the engines team at Ford's Dunton research centre. As the Ford people had little knowledge of Land Rover products and of their special needs, it was up to the Land Rover engineers to make sure those special needs were met. Among them was that there would have to be two different versions of the new engine to suit the Range Rover and the Range Rover Sport.

The main reason was the different physical configurations of the two vehicles. The Sport had a completely different mounting for the front differential from the one in the L322 Range Rover, and the sump had to be redesigned to suit this. The turbochargers had to be relocated about 100mm (4in) further back to suit the engine-bay packaging, and the front-end drive had to be redesigned to accommodate the pump for the Sport's anti-roll suspension. This was fitted in underneath the alternator, so the alternator had to move up and the Sport version of the TDV8 engine ended up with two belt drives instead of just one in the L322 derivative. In addition, the Sport's exhaust was specially tuned 'to give more of a rasp'.

The Dunton phase lasted for some six or eight months, and an important programme target was to make the new engine meet the EU4 emissions regulations that would become effective on 1 January 2007. The whole programme was then transferred to the Dagenham engine plant, where Ford put in their own engine programme manager, Roland Ernst, to oversee the transition to a production engine.

The normal Ford process at that time was to build three batches of engine prototypes, but with only two years left to meet the programme's targets, Grant Horne telescoped this down to just two batches. Experience from the V6 engine proved invaluable, and he commented:

We had a pretty good run through the development phases. No major problems showed up. There were some problems with thermal-mechanical stresses on the turbochargers, which cracked, but these were a design built on prototype tooling and so that wasn't very surprising! We didn't have any cylinder-head cracking problems, which you often get on new diesel engines. There were just small problems, like oil leaks from the cam covers and the sump. We had porosity of the sump as well. But we got on top of all the oil leaks.

The main differences between the first and later batches were in the breathing system, and affected the intake manifold, throttle position and the positions of the EGR coolers. These were relocated from the backs of the cylinder heads to inside the vee, giving both more compact packaging and better mixing of intake gases. Some bottom-end changes made the engine easier to manufacture, and the original sump design was changed for one that gave better noise, vibration and harshness (NVH) properties and reduced the risk of leaks.

Once the development phase had ended in early 2005, preparation of the cylinder-block tooling took another nine months. Everything was ready by the engineering sign-off target date of November 2005, and the next stage was a 250-strong pilot-production batch for validation testing, assembled on the same line as the V6 diesels at Dagenham. The first full production engine was completed in April 2006, and over the next four months production engines were tested in vehicles; the first production Range Rover TDV8 was completed on schedule in August, and the first Sport TDV8 (with serial number 988098) was completed in October.

THE 2007 MODELS

The new TDV8 Sport became available in the showrooms from November 2006 as a 2007 model, and was an immediate hit. In Europe (it was not made available in the USA or the Middle East) it rapidly became the engine of choice and more or less demolished sales of the naturally aspirated petrol V8, which was thirstier and could not match its torque and acceleration. Nevertheless, sales of the less expensive TDV6 models remained strong, and out-sold those with the larger diesel engine.

Land Rover had made sure that the TDV8 model looked the part of the high-performance diesel. It came with 20in wheels as standard, and with the same Titan-finish grille and side vents used on the Supercharged models – although its Land Rover logos were in the traditional gold on green rather than silver on black. There were Brembo brakes and the Dynamic Response system as used on the Supercharged models, and the TDV8 models also came with the Positive Torque gearbox control system from the Supercharged variants, which automatically blipped the throttle during downshifting to reduce shift times.

Like the other 2007 models, the TDV8 had a tailgate that was easier to open than before, thanks to a revised pivot point. It was easier to close, too, with a power-operated latch that pulled it down for the final short distance. Across the

range, a slightly revised range of paint colours was accompanied by some changes to the interior choices. Premium leather became an option for Supercharged models, and was also made available as part of the Ebony and Ivory colourway, while Straight Grain Walnut replaced the earlier Cherry Wood contrast trim option. All the instrument bezels now took on a bright painted finish, and the horn buttons, Terrain Response control, cubby-box release handle and hinge covers now came with what Land Rover called a Noble finish.

Further additions were a one-shot function for the front passenger's window, and in Europe and the UK only, the satellite navigation could now be programmed while the vehicle was moving. (On earlier models, it had been locked for safety reasons, but of course there was never any reason why a passenger should not operate it while the vehicle was being driven.) All leather-upholstered front seats gained a useful pocket on the vertical surface of the cushion, and a powered lumbar support adjuster was added to the Memory Pack seat option. In Europe, the UK and North America a tyre-pressure monitoring system now became standard: this used monitors on each wheel and miniature radio transmitters that would send a warning signal to the dashboard if a pressure drop of 25 per cent was detected in any one tyre.

Much less visible than all this were new 18in and 19in alloy wheels, which looked exactly like the earlier ones but

ABOVE: **This close-up picture is of a TDV8 model, with the same silver grille bars as the Supercharged types, but with a standard green and gold Land Rover logo.**

New for 2007 was Straight Grain Walnut contrast trim, seen here with Alpaca upholstery.

were actually considerably lighter. A reduction in weight of 3.25kg (7.16lb) on each 18in wheel and 2.77kg (6.1lb) on each 19in wheel made for worthwhile reductions in unsprung weight and actually contributed to an improvement in the ride quality on those models that had these wheel sizes.

Then, of course, there were changes in the vast list of accessories available for the Sport. The new Fender Vent option brought chromed side vents with a moulded grille behind them. The Stormer Accessories Pack made the HST-style bodykit available – and could be had ready painted if one of the 2006-model HST colours was required. A hybrid analogue-and-digital TV option acknowledged the increasing availability of digital TV signals; and lastly there was a set of G4 Challenge accessories. Inspired by the 2006 adventure challenge event, this added 'macho style' to the Sport, according to the 2007 sales brochure. The set consisted of an electric winch, an underbody protection shield, a raised air intake, an expedition roof rack, a rear access ladder, and a small G4 decal for each front door.

There was more: door-mirror covers were now available in body colour or in chrome, and a rear bumper tread plate branded 'Sport' could also be had. At the front end, a 'bumper styling cover' replaced the earlier A-frame option, probably because a softer appearance was considered more acceptable at a time when large 4×4 vehicles were coming under fire from various interest groups. The waterproof seat covers

were now offered in Aspen or Sand as well as the original grey, and a new audio connectivity system allowed an iPod to be integrated into the vehicle's built-in sound system. Acknowledging perhaps that the Sport had become a highly desirable vehicle and therefore more than usually prone to theft, a Land Rover Watch tracking system became available in late 2006.

A European Special Edition

During the 2007 model-year, a special Stormer edition was made available in France and Belgium. This appears to have been a diesel model with the Stormer bodykit used on the 2006 Supercharged HST edition in Britain.

Colour and Trim Options, 2007 Models

There were twelve paint options for the 2007 model-year. Atacama Sand, Lugano Teal and Stornoway Grey were all new; Bonatti Grey had gone. All these paints were metallic types except for Chawton White, which was a traditional 'solid' type.

The four upholstery colours remained unchanged from the previous model-year. There were two 'standard' contrast trim options, Straight Grain Walnut replacing the original Cherry Wood; Lined Oak was also available for the HST

Seen on a 2007 model, these were the functions that were easily accessible through the touch screen on the dashboard.

Choosing the 4×4 Info option provided this set of graphics. The transmission is in high range (Hi) and park (P), but it was fascinating to watch the movement of the suspension on the right-hand picture when the vehicle was moving slowly in rough terrain.

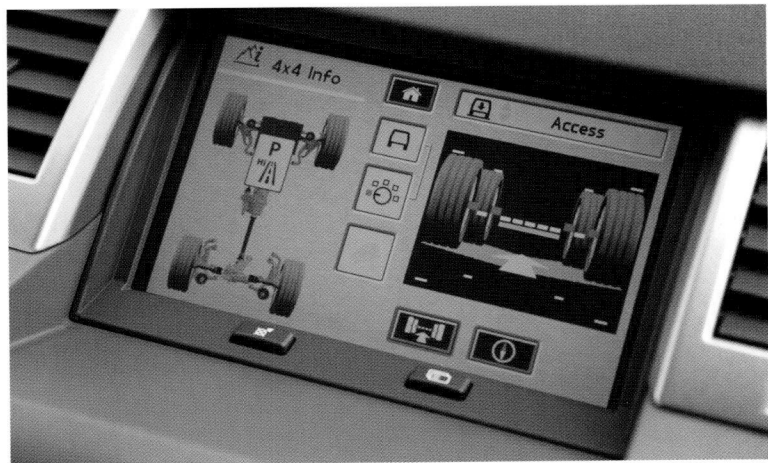

WHAT THE PRESS THOUGHT

Of the new TDV8 engine, *Land Rover Enthusiast* magazine suggested in its November 2006 issue that it 'makes the naturally aspirated petrol V8 completely redundant'. Not very many months later, that engine would actually be withdrawn from sale in Europe for precisely this reason.

Top Gear magazine of 10 January 2007 tried a TDV8 model and reported that:

> Zero to 60mph passes in an indecent 8.6sec, and in-gear responsiveness is so great that certain increments are dealt with faster than in the less torquey, but ultimately more powerful, supercharged RRS.... Many of the differences between the two are difficult to sense. Only the slightest vibration can be felt through the TDV8's throttle pedal, noise is well suppressed, and revs can be allowed to pile on happily without a steep cut-off in the engine's hunger to pull – unusually for a diesel.

Perhaps regretting its earlier, somewhat disparaging review of the Supercharged model, the AA's *Motoring* magazine for August 2007 noted that the Range Rover Sport was a 'smart, safe and speedy way to shift a family from A to B …an excellent choice', although it had reservations about 'surprisingly limited legroom in the rear'. It also accepted that 'Land Rover was on to a winner when it added the more affordable Range Rover Sport to its line-up to accompany the enduring Range Rover'. The review noted that the TDV8 was 'considerably more expensive than the V6 option, but the newer engine makes bludgeoning a path across any surface a relaxing and enjoyable experience'.

models only. Most combinations were feasible, although Land Rover did refuse to provide some combinations that they considered did not work; in sales catalogues they also highlighted the ones they thought worked best by describing them as 'designer's choice' options.

Premium leather was softer than standard leather and was ruched. Sports leather had perforations, through which a bright metallic backing was visible.

CARPETS
The combinations were dependent on the upholstery colour, and were as follows:

With Alpaca upholstery:	Ebony carpets
With Aspen upholstery:	Aspen carpets
With Ebony upholstery:	Ebony carpets
With Ivory upholstery:	Aspen or Ebony carpets

Rimini Red suited the Sport's lines and image, but was surprisingly rare in Britain. This is a TDV8 model.

COLOUR AND TRIM OPTIONS

Paint	Codes	Notes
Arctic Frost	962, MBH	Designer's choice with Aspen upholstery and Straight Grain Walnut trim
Atacama Sand	916, NAU	Designer's choices were Alpaca, Aspen or Ivory upholstery with Straight Grain Walnut trim
Buckingham Blue	796, JGJ	Designer's choice with Ivory upholstery and Lined Oak trim
Cairns Blue	849, JEU	Not available with Aspen upholstery
Chawton White	603, NAL	
Giverny Green	734, HZB	Designer's choice with Aspen or Ivory upholstery and Straight Grain Walnut trim
Java Black	697, PNF	Designer's choices were Alpaca, Ebony or Ivory upholstery with Lined Oak trim
Lugano Teal	963, JMB	Not available with Aspen upholstery. Designer's choices were Ebony or Ivory upholstery with Lined Oak trim
Rimini Red	889, CBK	Not available with Aspen or Ivory upholstery. Designer's choices were Alpaca upholstery with Lined Oak trim and Ebony upholstery with Rhodium trim
Stornoway Grey	907, LEL	Designer's choices were Ebony or Ivory upholstery with Lined Oak trim
Tonga Green	904, HFY	Designer's choices were Alpaca upholstery with Lined Oak trim, and Ivory upholstery with Straight Grain Walnut trim
Zambezi Silver	737, MVC	Designer's choices were Ebony or Ivory upholstery with Lined Oak trim

UPHOLSTERY OPTIONS

Specification	Material	Colour options
S	Cloth	Alpaca, Ebony
SE	Leather	Alpaca, Aspen, Ebony
HSE	Premium leather	Alpaca, Ebony, Ivory
Supercharged	Sports leather	Ebony, Ivory

WHEEL AND TYRE OPTIONS, 2007 MODEL-YEAR

Specification	Description
S	17in with five split spokes and 235/65R17 tyres
	Optional 18in with ten spokes and 255/55R18 tyres
SE	18in with five split spokes and 255/55R18 tyres
	Optional 19in with five V-spokes and 255/50R19 tyres
HSE	19in with five V-spokes and 255/50R19 tyres
Supercharged	20in with ten spokes and 275/40R20 tyres

CONTRAST PANEL OPTIONS

The standard contrast panels were Rhodium, but Straight Grain Walnut was optional at no extra cost. Lined Oak was available only on HST models.

2008: A YEAR OF CHANGE AND UNCERTAINTY

The year 2008 had been planned as a celebration year for Land Rover, because it was the sixtieth anniversary of the marque. But that sixtieth anniversary was celebrated against a background of economic uncertainty on the one hand, and one of major business change on the other. It was little wonder that in December 2008 Land Rover cancelled the G4 Challenge event planned for 2009. The financial future was too uncertain to take the risk of such major publicity expense, and the company chose instead to focus its resources on the new and more eco-friendly models that it needed in the short and medium term.

The major business change saw Land Rover up for sale in the early part of 2008, along with its stable-mate Jaguar. This was the culmination of a series of events that had begun with Ford returning some disastrous financial results for 2005; by early 2007 the American company had drawn up plans to sell off elements of its European operations. Ford began to examine offers to buy Jaguar and Land Rover in July 2007; by September the Indian Tata group had entered the picture, and by January 2008, Tata had become the preferred bidder. On 26 March 2008 Ford announced it had concluded a definitive agreement to sell both Jaguar and Land Rover to Tata.

The deal was completed on 2 June 2008; the price was $2.3 billion. As things were to turn out, Tata would prove to be a strong and committed 'parent' for the Land Rover marque, but there were certainly those who feared the opposite in 2008 – and among them were many who worked for Land Rover.

The deal is done: Ford and Land Rover representatives sign Land Rover over to Ratan Tata of the Tata Group, along with Jaguar.

A Sport (nearest the camera here) figured on the Gerry Judah sculpture that accompanied Land Rover's headline sponsorship of the 2008 Goodwood Festival of Speed. The sculpture was commissioned as part of the company's sixtieth anniversary celebrations, and was called 'Breadth of Capability' – a Land Rover catch-phrase of the time. The Sport was a real one, but it had been made lighter by having most of its interior removed, and quite possibly the engine too.

THE 2008 MODELS

The 2008 model-year had started optimistically enough in September 2007. The TDV8 models had secured themselves a strong position in the middle of the Sport range, and in Britain and most of Europe the poor-selling naturally aspirated V8 models were dropped from the range altogether.

This must have freed up engine supplies for North America and the Middle East, where the 4.4-litre V8 remained the favourite engine.

So the 2008 Sport line-up in Britain consisted of TDV6, TDV8 and Supercharged models. There were still S, SE, HSE and Supercharged trim levels, but the S was now only available with the TDV6 engine; the SE and HSE could be had with the TDV6 or TDV8 diesels; and the Supercharged model had its own high trim and equipment specification. Sales were strong globally, and Land Rover clearly felt that there was no real need to overhaul the Sport's specification to a very great extent for 2008.

So the changes were minimal, with a few routine substitutions in the list of paint options, and an option to have the door handles painted to match the body. There was a slightly more extensive set of changes for the interior, where Brunel contrast trim replaced Rhodium as the standard fit, Straight Grain Walnut remained a no-cost option, and Dark Zebrano was introduced as a second no-cost option. For the Premium ruched leather, Tan was introduced as a fourth colour. Even the accessories list was barely altered, the main change being availability of what was called the Snow Traction System – a set of snow chains that were adjustable to fit all the sizes of wheel now available on the Sport as standard (the earlier snow-chain set had not fitted 17in or 20in wheels).

A Second HST

However, a plan was firmly in place to brighten up the 2008 model-year as the celebrations for Land Rover's sixtieth anniversary got under way, and in March 2008 Land Rover introduced two new limited-volume models. The more glamorous of these was another HST model, and in preparation for it the mainstream supercharged model had been renamed a Super-charged HSE in December 2007. Alongside it, for what Land Rover called the 2008.5 model-year, was a new XS derivative, though this was available for a limited time period only.

The first HST in summer 2006 had established that the HST designation indicated performance combined with exclusive styling. The 2008 HST was available not only with the Supercharged engine as before, but also with the TDV8 diesel – a clear hint to the buying public that the big diesel stood for top levels of performance. With both engines, the HST had Dynamic Response suspension and Brembo brakes. The 20in Stormer wheels and bodykit of spoilers were the same as before, and so were the body-colour lower door

The sales catalogues for the 2008 model-year reflected the confidence and optimism that accompanied a record-breaking 2007.

BELOW LEFT: **This 2008 model proudly displays the TDV8 badge of the Sport's big diesel engine.**

The 2008 Sport **HST** came with privacy glass behind the B-pillars unless a customer requested otherwise. The bodykit was familiar, but this model could be had with the TDV8 engine as well as the supercharged one. Pictured is a TDV8 version, with gold-on-green grille badge.

and tailgate mouldings. This time, rear privacy glass was standard, although it could be deleted to special order.

There were no restrictions on the paint choices from the standard 2008 palette. Premium ruched leather was standard in any one of the four 2008 colours, but it was also possible to order these seats with Alcantara centre panels (in Alpaca or Ebony only), or to have Sports leather seats in Ebony or Ivory. Lined Oak trim made a comeback as the standard fit, but both Straight Grained Walnut and Stained Zebrano

(which appears to have been the same as Dark Zebrano) were optional.

There are no reliable figures for the number of HST models that were sold. Land Rover did not promote the HST as a limited edition but rather as 'the absolute pinnacle of the Range Rover Sport line-up', and no doubt the plan was always to sell as many as they could.

The UK XS Model

The second limited-volume model in March 2008 was called the XS, and was priced between the entry-level S and the SE. It was a TDV6 with Ebony leather and Brunel contrast trim, and there were just four exterior colour options: Java Black, Rimini Red, Stornoway Grey and Zermatt Silver.

'Outside are eye-catching 19in alloy wheels,' gushed the sales brochure (they were the V-spoke type). 'On the inside is Personal Telephone Integration, a Premium Navigation system, and, for added comfort and a true luxury feel, leather seat facings.' The target customers were those who might otherwise have bought an S model, and once again there is no information about volumes, although it appears that the XS was available only until April 2008. No doubt Land Rover again sold as many as demand allowed.

Colour and Trim Options, 2008 Models

There were twelve paint options for most of the 2008 model-year, although a few very early vehicles were finished in a pair of 2007 colours (Arctic Frost and Chawton White). These two colours were replaced during September 2007 by Izmir Blue and Alaska White. Lucerne Green replaced Giverny Green, and Zermatt Silver replaced Zambezi Silver. All these paints were metallic types except for Alaska White, which was a traditional 'solid' type.

There were now five upholstery colours, although one (Tan) was only available with Premium leather. The number of contrast trims was reduced to three. Most combinations were feasible, although Land Rover did refuse to provide some combinations that they considered did not work; in sales catalogues they also highlighted the ones they thought worked best by describing them as 'designer's choice' options.

Premium leather was softer than standard leather and was ruched. Sports leather had perforations, through which a bright metallic backing was visible.

CARPETS
The combinations were dependent on the upholstery colour. They were as follows:

With Alpaca upholstery:	Ebony carpets
With Aspen upholstery:	Aspen carpets
With Ebony upholstery:	Ebony carpets
With Ivory upholstery:	Aspen or Ebony carpets

The XS was a short-lived special model designed to boost sales at the bottom end of the Sport range.

COLOUR AND TRIM OPTIONS

Paint	Codes	Notes
Alaska White	909, NCL	
Arctic Frost	962, MBH	To September 2007 only. Designer's choice with Ebony upholstery and Dark Zebrano trim. Not available with Aspen/Ivory colourway
Atacama Sand	916, NAU	Designer's choices were Aspen upholstery with Straight Grain Walnut trim, and Ebony upholstery with Dark Zebrano trim
Buckingham Blue	796, JGJ	Designer's choice with Ebony upholstery and Dark Zebrano trim
Cairns Blue	849, JEU	Not available with Ebony/Tan or Aspen/Ivory with Ivory carpets
Chawton White	603, NAL	To September 2007 only
Izmir Blue	920, MWE	Designer's choice with Ebony/Alpaca and Dark Zebrano trim. Not available with Aspen/Ivory colourway
Java Black	697, PNF	Designer's choices were Ebony/Tan with Brunel trim, and Ebony with Stained Zebrano trim
Lucerne Green	966, HZV	Designer's choices were Aspen/Ivory with Straight Grain Walnut or Dark Zebrano trim
Lugano Teal	963, JMB	Not available with Aspen upholstery. Designer's choices were Ebony/Tan with Brunel trim, and Ebony/Ivory with Dark Zebrano trim
Rimini Red	889, CBK	Not available with Aspen or Ivory upholstery. Designer's choices were Ebony/Ebony with Dark Zebrano trim, and Ebony/Alpaca with Straight Grain Walnut trim
Stornoway Grey	907, LEL	Designer's choices were Ebony/Alpaca with Straight Grain Walnut trim, Ebony/Tan with Brunel trim, and Ebony/Ebony with Dark Zebrano trim
Tonga Green	904, HFY	Designer's choices were Aspen/Ivory and Ebony/Alpaca, both with Straight Grain Walnut trim
Zermatt Silver	798, MBK	Designer's choices were Ebony/Alpaca with Straight Grain Walnut trim, and Ebony/Ebony with Dark Zebrano trim

UPHOLSTERY OPTIONS

Specification	Material	Colour options
S	Cloth	Alpaca, Ebony
SE	Leather	Alpaca, Aspen, Ebony
HSE	Premium leather	Alpaca, Ebony, Ivory, Tan
Supercharged	Sports leather	Ebony, Ivory

WHEEL AND TYRE OPTIONS, 2008 MODEL-YEAR

Specification	
S	17in with five split spokes and 235/65R17 tyres
	Optional 18in with ten spokes and 255/55R18 tyres
SE	18in with ten spokes and 255/55R18 tyres
	Optional 19in with five V-spokes and 255/50R19 tyres
HSE	19in with five V-spokes and 255/50R19 tyres
Supercharged	20in with ten spokes and 275/40R20 tyres

CONTRAST PANEL OPTIONS

The standard contrast panels were Brunel, but Dark Zebrano and Straight Grain Walnut were optional at no extra cost.

Wheel and Tyre Options, 2008 Model-Year

Centre caps normally carried a gold-on-green Land Rover logo, but those for the Supercharged models were silver on black.

THE 2009 MODEL-YEAR: MORE GLOOM

The 2009 model-year Sport was sold against a backdrop of economic gloom and weakening demand, when sales of non-essential vehicles hit a brick wall. In Britain there were very few Range Rover Sports registered with the '09' and later '59' plates, although Jaguar Land Rover did register a larger than usual number themselves for use as company cars to be sold into the market after a year's use by JLR employees. In Britain, the company held its collective breath, hoping to stimulate sales with a mid-season limited edition.

A few changes had been in the pipeline and were implemented as the model-year opened in autumn 2008. Three new paint colours were introduced, replacing two earlier ones; all three of them were shared with the Discovery 3, for which they were also new. Interiors were freshened up with the introduction of Almond in place of Alpaca for the light beige option, and for the HSE and Supercharged models it was now possible to order Premium seats with Alcantara wearing surfaces instead of the ruched leather. A wider choice of interior colour and contrast panel combinations became available, although the description in the sales catalogues of a limited number as 'designer's choices' no doubt guided customer orders and helped to limit complication on the assembly lines!

There were some changes to the wheel options, too. Essentially, the three lower specification levels all moved up one size, so that the S level now had 18in wheels (instead of 17in), the SE came with 19in (instead of 18in) and the HSE with 20in (instead of 19in). As for the Supercharged models, the Stormer wheels formerly reserved for special editions such as the HST now became standard wear. The slow-selling and expensive two-piece 20in wheels disappeared from the accessories catalogue, to be replaced by three new designs that included Shadow Chrome and diamond-turned finishes. These larger wheels were what the customers wanted, but Land Rover was in no doubt that they had disadvantages. In sales catalogues they added the note that 'wheels with larger diameters and lower profile tyres may offer certain styling or driving benefits, but may be more vulnerable to damage.'

ABOVE LEFT AND RIGHT: **The sales brochures for the 2009 model-year seemed to reflect the sombre mood that prevailed at Land Rover. Without digital enhancement it would be impossible to read the shadow-black lettering on these two covers!**

Land Rover registered a good number of Sports for its own use during the currency of the '09' registration plate in Britain, reasoning that they would create a healthy second-hand stock when trading conditions returned to normal. This one, in the Zermatt Silver introduced for 2008 and still available, belonged to the Land Rover Experience demonstrations team and was pictured at an exhibition at London's Canary Wharf.

BELOW: **For 2009, Almond replaced Alpaca as an interior colour, and was accompanied on leather seats by contrast stitching in Nutmeg.**

Ivory contrast stitching was used with Ebony leather, and this vehicle has the new Noble contrast trim as well.

BELOW LEFT: **The four contrast trims for 2009 are seen here, including the new diamond-stitched leather type.**

PREMIUM LEATHER INSERT STRAIGHT GRAIN WALNUT

The Stormer Edition

The mid-season boost to sales of the Sport in Britain took the shape of a 300-strong Stormer Edition, which was previewed at the Boat Show in January 2009. It was designed as a value-for-money prospect, with a lot of extra equipment loaded on to an SE-specification TDV6 model.

That extra equipment included the Stormer bodykit from the accessories range, plus 20in wheels, body-coloured side mouldings and lower tailgate, leather upholstery, front and rear parking sensors and pre-wiring for a Bluetooth mobile phone installation. The Stormer Edition went on sale in March 2009 in just three colours – Alaska White, Santorini

Black and Stornoway Grey – and was priced at £43,550, which positioned it slightly above the £43,095 TDV6 SE model.

European Special Editions

There were two special editions for continental Europe during the 2009 model-year, both probably intended to boost sales during the period of global recession.

BLACK & WHITE EDITION

The Black & White Edition was made available in France and Germany in October 2008, and possibly also in other countries. There were sixty examples for France and 200 for Germany. These models were characterized by privacy glass behind the B-pillars, and by 20in, ten-spoke wheels with a Chrome Shadow finish.

TECHNIUM EDITION

Land Rover France had used the 'Technium' name for special editions of several models since 2002. The Range Rover Sport Technium Edition became available in April 2009, and was essentially a package of upgrades added to existing models. S models had Bi-Xenon lights, the Visibility Pack, rear

The 2009 model-year brought a greater variety of 20in wheels. A Sparkle Silver finish was standard, but the ones illustrated at top centre have a diamond-turned finish, and those at bottom left a shadow chrome finish.

The Stormer Edition gave a boost to sales in March 2009, adding the familiar angular bodykit and other items to an entry-level TDV6 model.

park distance control, leather upholstery and Bluetooth connectivity in addition to the standard specification.

SE models had front park distance control, power-adjusted door mirrors, chromed sill plates, Premium carpet, leather and Alcantara upholstery, Bluetooth connectivity, and an eight-speaker harmon/kardon ICE system connectivity in addition to the standard specification.

HSE models had rear privacy glass, Premium leather upholstery, a rear DVD system, a LOGIC 7 ICE system with thirteen speakers, and Bluetooth connectivity in addition to the standard specification.

Supercharged models (rare in France anyway) had no package of extras, but were instead reduced in price during the availability of the Technium Edition.

The 2009 G4 Challenge Vehicles

Land Rover planned to run a third G4 Challenge event in 2009, and began recruiting contestants in February 2008. A key element of the 2009 Challenge was that it would raise money for the International Federation of Red Cross and Red Crescent Societies, which Land Rover had pledged to support in September 2007. However, the event was cancelled in December 2008 in the face of the global economic downturn and its effects on Land Rover's profitability.

However, a number of vehicles had already been built in preparation for the event. Among these were eight 2009-model Range Rover Sports, two with TDV6 engines and six with the TDV8. Probably all had the HSE specification. They were painted in the familiar G4 Challenge colour of Tangiers Orange, and most (possibly all) were fitted with the full complement of G4 Challenge equipment. That meant a Warn 9000XP front winch, Goodyear MT/R tyres, a roofrack, Hella Xenon auxiliary roof lights, steering and fuel-tank guards made by Mantec, and internal load guards.

Three of these vehicles actually saw use in connection with the planned event. One was used as a publicity vehicle during the event recce in Mongolia during 2008, and the other two were used during national selection events for the Belgian, British and Irish teams. After the event was cancelled, the Sports were sold off; most are thought still to exist in private ownership.

Colour and Trim Options, 2009 Models

There were thirteen paint options for the 2009 model-year, of which three were new. These were Bournville, Galway Green and Santorini Black. Java Black and Tonga Green were no longer available. All these paints were metallic types except for Alaska White, which was a traditional 'solid' type. Bournville was also described as a 'pearlescent' paint.

There were again five upholstery colours, although one (Tan) was only available with Premium leather. Trim finishers and door contrast panels were now treated separately, and there was a new and complex matrix of options. Most combinations were available, although Land Rover did refuse to provide some combinations that they considered did not work; in sales catalogues they also highlighted the ones they thought worked best by describing them as 'designer's choice' options.

The table opposite uses Land Rover's interior option codes for clarity and to save space. The codes were as follows:

TAC	Ivory Premium leather with Aspen carpet
TCA	Ebony cloth with Ebony carpet
TCB	Ebony Premium leather with Ebony carpet
TCH	Aspen leather with Aspen carpet
TCL	Ebony leather with Ebony carpet
TCQ	Ebony Sports leather with Ebony carpet
TDA	Ivory Premium leather with Ebony carpet
TDB	Ivory Sports leather with Ebony carpet
TEN	Tan Premium leather with Ebony carpet (not available with diagonal stitched inserts)
TEZ	Ebony leather and Lunar Alcantara with Ebony carpet
TFJ	Almond leather with Nutmeg carpet
TFK	Almond leather and Nutmeg Alcantara with Nutmeg carpet
TFL	Almond Premium leather with Nutmeg carpet

Contrast stitching was an option with Ebony leather only.

Premium leather was softer than standard leather and was ruched. Almond Premium leather had contrast stitching in Nutmeg, and Ebony Premium leather had stitching in Ivory. Sports leather had perforations, through which a bright metallic backing was visible. The leather and Alcantara option had plain leather for the bolsters and Alcantara for the insert panels; Lunar Alcantara went with Ebony leather, and Nutmeg Alcantara with Almond leather.

CONTRAST PANEL OPTIONS

S and SE models: Brunel was standard for the trim finishers. Diagonal-stitched door insert panels were standard for the S, and Straight Grain Walnut for the SE. There were no options for the S, but diagonal-stitched and Dark Zebrano inserts were both available for the SE.

HSE, Supercharged and HST models: Noble was standard for the trim finishers. Diagonal-stitched door insert panels were standard for the Supercharged models; Dark Zebrano was standard for the HSE; and Lined Oak for the HST. Straight Grain Walnut was an option for all these models, while Dark Zebrano was optional for the Supercharged and HST types; Premium leather inserts were optional for the HSE and HST models.

Wheel and Tyre Options, 2009 Model-Year

Centre caps normally carried a gold-on-green Land Rover logo, but those for the Supercharged models were silver on black.

COLOUR AND TRIM OPTIONS

Paint	Codes	Availability
Alaska White	909, NCL	All combinations available
Atacama Sand	916, NAU	All combinations available. Designer's choices: TAC with Straight Grain Walnut; TDA or TDB with Dark Zebrano
Bournville	822. AAD	TAC and TCH not available. Designer's choices: TEN with Premium leather inserts; TFJ, TFK or TFL with Dark Zebrano inserts
Buckingham Blue	796, JGJ	All combinations available. Designer's choice: TDA with Dark Zebrano inserts
Cairns Blue	849, JEU	TCH and TEN not available
Galway Green	821, HAC	All combinations available. Designer's choices: TAC, TFJ, TFK or TFL with Straight Grain Walnut
Izmir Blue	920, MWE	TAC and TCH not available. Designer's choices: TFJ, TFK or TFL with Dark Zebrano inserts; TCA, TCB, TCL, TCQ or TEZ with Lined Oak inserts
Lucerne Green	966, HZV	All combinations available. Designer's choices: TCH or TFK with Straight Grain Walnut inserts; TAC or TEZ with Dark Zebrano inserts
Lugano Teal	963, JMB	TCH not available. Designer's choices: TDA or TDB with Dark Zebrano inserts
Rimini Red	889, CBK	TAC and TCH not available. Designer's choices: TFJ or TFL with Straight Grain Walnut inserts; TCA, TCB, TCL, TCQ or TFK with Dark Zebrano inserts; TDA, TDB or TEZ with Lined Oak inserts
Santorini Black	820, PAB	All combinations available. Designer's choices: TEN with Premium Leather inserts; TFK with Straight Grain Walnut; TCA, TCB, TCL, TCQ or TEZ with Dark Zebrano inserts; TDA or TDB with Lined Oak inserts
Stornoway Grey	907, LEL	All combinations available. Designer's choices: TFJ, TFK or TFL with Straight Grain Walnut inserts; TCA, TCB, TCL, TCQ or TEZ with Dark Zebrano inserts; TDA or TDB with Lined Oak inserts
Zermatt Silver	798, MBK	All combinations available. Designer's choices: TFJ, TFK or TFL with Straight Grain Walnut inserts; TCA, TCB, TCL, TCQ or TEZ with Dark Zebrano inserts; TDA or TDB with Lined Oak inserts

UPHOLSTERY TYPE OPTIONS

Specification	Material	Colour options
S	Cloth	Ebony
SE	Leather	Almond, Aspen, Ebony
HSE	Premium leather	Almond, Ebony, Ivory, Tan
	Leather and Alcantara	
Supercharged	Sports leather	Ebony, Ivory
	Leather and Alcantara	Almond, Ebony

WHEEL AND TYRE OPTIONS, 2009 MODEL-YEAR

Specification	Description
S	18in × 8J with ten spokes and 255/55R18 tyres
SE	19in × 9J with five V-spokes, Sparkle Silver finish and 255/50R19 tyres
HSE	20in × 9.5J with ten spokes, Sparkle Silver finish and 275/40R20 tyres
Supercharged	20in × 9.5J Stormer with nine spokes, Titan Silver finish and 275/40R20 tyres
Accessory	20in × 9.5J with ten spokes, Shadow Chrome finish and 275/40R20 tyres
Accessory	20in × 9.5J fifteen-spoke with Sparkle Silver finish and 275/40R20 tyres
Accessory	20in × 9.5J fifteen-spoke with diamond-turned finish and 275/40R20 tyres

Option Pack system

For the 2009 model-year, Land Rover also introduced an Option Pack system. This grouped some of the most popular options into a series of packages, so making choices easier for customers and reducing complication on the assembly lines. There were seven Option Packs, as follows:

Clear View Pack: Front fog lamps, headlamp washers, automatic headlamps, rain sensor, electrochromatic (self-dipping) rear view mirror. (Suitable for the S models only, because all this equipment was already standard on the others.)

Cold Climate Pack: Heated windscreen, heated washer jets, and heated front and rear seats. (All this equipment was standard on Supercharged models.)

Dynamic Pack: 20in ten-spoke or Stormer wheels, Dynamic Response system, Brembo brakes, and Bi-Xenon headlamps. (Not available on TDV8 or Supercharged models.)

Technical Specifications, 2007–2009

Engines

(1) TDV6 2.7-litre diesel
2720cc (81 × 88mm) Ford-Peugeot ohv V6 diesel with 4
  valves per cylinder, common-rail injection, turbocharger and
  intercooler (to EU4 emissions standards)
Siemens PDC2 engine-management system
18:1 compression ratio
190bhp at 4,000rpm
325lb/ft at 1,900rpm

(2) 4.4-litre Jaguar V8 petrol
4394cc (88 × 90.3) Jaguar AJ-8 petrol V8 with four camshafts
  and 4 valves per cylinder
Denso EMS generation 1 engine-management system
10.75:1 compression ratio
300bhp at 5,500rpm
315lb/ft at 4,000rpm

(3) 4.2-litre Supercharged V8 petrol
4197cc (86 × 90.3mm) Jaguar AJ-8 petrol V8 with four
  camshafts and 4 valves per cylinder, plus Eaton supercharger
  and intercooler
Denso EMS generation 1 engine-management system
9.1:1 compression ratio
390bhp at 5,750rpm
410lb/ft at 3,500rpm

(4) 3.6-litre TDV8 diesel
3630cc (81 × 88mm) Ford-Land Rover ohv V8 diesel
  with 4 valves per cylinder, common-rail injection, twin
  turbochargers and intercooler
17.3:1 compression ratio
268bhp at 4,000rpm
472lb/ft at 2,000rpm

Transmission
Permanent four-wheel drive with centre differential
  incorporating viscous coupling to give automatic locking;
  Terrain Response traction system standard; optional locking
  rear differential

Final drive ratio: 3.73:1 (V8 petrol models)
  3.54:1 (TDV6, TDV8 and V8 supercharged
  models)

Primary gearbox:
Six-speed ZF 6HP26 automatic; ratios 4.171:1, 2.340:1,
  1.521:1, 1.143:1, 0.867:1, 0.691:1, reverse 3.403:1

Transfer gearbox:
Separate two-speed type with 'active' centre differential; high
  ratio 1:1, low ratio 2.93:1

Hi ICE Pack: Harmon/kardon ICE system with eight speakers, passive sub-woofer audio amplifier, and in-dash 6×CD autochanger. (All this equipment was standard on HSE models and above.)

Memory Pack: Memory for seats and door mirrors with three settings for the driver; power lumbar support adjustment for the driver's seat. (All this equipment was standard on HSE models and above.)

Premium ICE Pack: Harmon/kardon LOGIC 7 ICE system with thirteen speakers, active subwoofer, DSP amplifier, and rear headphone module. (All this equipment was standard on Supercharged models.)

Tow Pack: Fixed-height swan-neck tow hitch (or receiver) and electrics.

Suspension
Independent front and rear suspension with height-adjustable electronic air suspension and telescopic dampers; double wishbones front and rear

Steering
ZF Servotronic speed-proportional power-assisted rack and pinion

Brakes
Four-wheel disc brakes with dual hydraulic line, servo assistance and Bosch four-channel ABS
Ventilated front discs with 317mm diameter (TDV6), 337mm diameter (4.4V8) or 360mm diameter (supercharged V8), with four-piston callipers
Ventilated rear discs with 325mm diameter single-pot callipers (TDV6 and V8 models) or 350mm diameter and four-piston callipers (supercharged V8 and TDV8)
Servo-operated parking brake operating on drums within the rear discs

Vehicle Dimensions

Wheelbase:	2,745mm (108.1in)
Overall length:	4,788mm (188.5in)
Overall width:	1,928mm (75.9in); 2,170mm (85.4in) over mirrors

Overall height:	1,817mm (71.5in) at standard ride height
Unladen weight (for typical UK-market models):	(1) 2.7-litre diesel models: 2,455kg (5,412lb)
	(2) 4.4-litre petrol models: 2,480kg (5,468lb)
	(3) 4.2-litre Supercharged V8 models: 2,572kg (5,670lb)
	(4) 3.6-litre TDV8 models: 2,656–2,756kg (5,855–6,076lb)

Performance

(1) 2.7-litre TDV6 models

Max. speed:	120mph (193km/h)
0–60mph:	11.9sec

(2) 4.4-litre petrol V8 models

Max. speed:	130mph (209km/h)
0–60mph:	8.2sec

(3) 4.2-litre V8 Supercharged models

Max. speed:	140mph (225km/h)
0–60mph:	7.2sec

(4) 3.6-litre TDV8 models

Max. speed:	130mph (210km/h)
0–60mph:	8.6sec

CHAPTER FIVE

MORE 'PREMIUM': THE 2010 MODELS

The 2009 global recession could hardly have come at a worse time for Jaguar Land Rover. The company had been planning a major new-model programme for both its brands, to begin with Jaguars in January 2009 and continue with Land Rovers in June. The two brands were to share new engines, and the company had already committed to those by the time the recession really began to bite.

Whether the option of postponing the new-model launches was ever seriously considered at JLR's Whitley headquarters is not clear. One way or another, though, the company clearly decided to grit its teeth and get on with the job, in the hope that the recession would blow over by the end of 2009. Indeed it did – according to the US National Bureau of Economic Research, it ended in June 2009 – but consumer confidence took a lot longer to return.

DEVELOPMENT OF THE 2010 MODELS

Despite the changes that had taken place within Land Rover since the Range Rover Sport had been developed in the early 2000s, there was a welcome continuity as work began on the revised L320 that would be introduced in mid-2009 for the 2010 model-year. Stuart Frith remained in place as Chief Programme Engineer, and it was his task to guide the development of the new models.

From the start, Land Rover had some fairly well identified aims in developing the 2010-model Range Rover Sport. The early versions of the model had been a bigger success than they had expected, making clear that L320 as originally conceived was meeting customer demands – and, as JLR sales material regularly boasted, exceeding their expectations as well. So the second-series L320 was developed to have

more of the features that had given the first-series cars their appeal. It was to have more performance, and it was to have more luxury. Overall, it was to be – as Land Rover spokespersons loved to explain – more 'premium'. One result of this policy was that the entry-level S trim was dropped, and a new top-level Autobiography was pioneered at the end of the model-year.

ENGINE DEVELOPMENT

The merging of Jaguar and Land Rover in 2005 had led to Jaguar taking the lead in the development of new engines, although Land Rover retained its own engines development team, which worked with Jaguar on new designs, and also adapted them to suit the special requirements of Land Rovers. In particular, these special requirements related to lubrication systems – which had to operate satisfactorily at extreme angles in off-road use that no Jaguar would ever encounter – and to the dust-proofing that was essential to guarantee fault-free operation in some of the world's drier climates. Actual manufacture of the engines was, of course, carried out at the Ford plants in Bridgend and Dagenham, and this would remain the case until the end of Range Rover Sport production in 2013.

Of the engines in production for the Range Rover Sport as the 2009 model-year came to an end, only the 3.6-litre TDV8 diesel was left unchanged. Unique to Land Rover models (the Sport and the full-size Range Rover), it had been introduced in 2006 for the 2007 model-year and was therefore still fresh enough to need no major work. However, the smaller-capacity TDV6 diesel was extensively modified and emerged as a 3.0-litre engine, which replaced the 2.7-litre engine for all major markets – although a few others continued to take

2.7-litre TDV6 models during the 2010 model-year. The two petrol V8s were redeveloped around a common 5.0-litre size.

Most important was that all these new engines had to be shared with Jaguar models, and so a high priority was put on common componentry; this was the first time that new engines had been designed from the outset with the requirements of both brands in mind.

The 3.0-litre TDV6

The 2.7-litre V6 diesel that Ford had developed in tandem with Peugeot-Citroën was used in both Jaguar saloons and in Land Rovers (the Discovery 3 and Range Rover Sport), but the two versions of the engine had some major differences. Where the Land Rover versions had a single turbocharger and developed 190bhp, the Jaguar versions had twin turbochargers and a power output of 204bhp. Land Rover called their version the TDV6, while the Jaguar engine was known as the AJD-V6 (Advanced Jaguar Diesel V6).

Jaguar needed a new and more powerful version of this engine for introduction in their planned new XF saloon, which would replace the S-Type in January 2009. Land Rover needed a more powerful version to enhance their revised range scheduled for summer 2010 – the Discovery 4 and second-series Range Rover Sport. So the development

programme for this engine focused on three main targets: higher performance, greater commonality between Jaguar and Land Rover versions, and compliance with the new EU5 emissions regulations that were to come into force for all cars sold after 1 January 2011.

Although the basic architecture of the V6 diesel engine remained unchanged, its block was redesigned with bigger bores and a longer stroke to give a swept volume of close to 3.0 litres. In the interests of commonality, the decision was made that both Jaguar and Land Rover versions of the engine should have twin turbochargers. However, this time those turbochargers were given a parallel sequential arrangement, the first of its kind to be fitted to a V engine. Most of the time, the engine used only the larger primary turbocharger, which was a variable-geometry type, and the smaller secondary turbo remained out of circuit. But above 2,500rpm, the secondary turbocharger was brought into play within 300 milliseconds, seamlessly boosting the power delivery in the upper rev ranges where the earlier 2.7-litre engine had been disappointing in its Land Rover form.

The new 3.0-litre TDV6 engine gained third-generation common-rail injection with piezo injectors and fuel metering, which lowered its CO_2 emissions by a claimed 8.3 per cent over the 2.7-litre engine, to 243g/km. This more precise use of fuel also helped to reduce the actual use of fuel, and a lower idling speed also made its contribution to that. For those countries with tighter emissions regulations

This Stornoway Grey vehicle was built in May 2009 as a pre-production example for the 2010 model-year with the new 3.0-litre TDV6 engine.

already in place, a diesel particulates filter was fitted without harm to the power output, and was planned for use on all models when the new EU5 regulations became effective in Europe.

With a Bosch Generation 3 engine-management system in place of the Siemens type on the 2.7-litre engine, the improvements were simply enormous. In its Land Rover form for the Range Rover Sport, the engine delivered 245bhp, or 29 per cent more power than the earlier TDV6. Torque made a similarly impressive leap, peaking with 442lb/ft (36 per cent up) but delivering far more useful improvements further down the rev range, which made the new engine supremely flexible. Engine response was also very much improved, and Land Rover claimed that the 3.0-litre TDV6 could deliver 500Nm of torque within 500 milliseconds, so giving instantaneous access to 83 per cent of the maximum torque available.

With such specifications, the new 3.0-litre TDV6 diesel made the TDV8 more or less redundant as a Range Rover Sport option for most markets. Nevertheless, although it disappeared from the options lists in most European countries, it remained available where there was customer demand. It also remained the only diesel option for the full-size Range Rover – and in the meantime a development programme was planned to enlarge it to 4.4 litres in time to meet more new emissions regulations.

ABOVE LEFT: **The new 3.0-litre TDV6 engine with two parallel sequential turbochargers was central to the revised 2010 range in diesel-oriented markets.**

This remarkable cutaway shows the layout of the twin turbochargers and their intercooler.

The V8 Petrol Engines

Like the programme to develop the 3.0-litre diesel V6 engine, one of the key aims of the programme to develop the naturally aspirated and supercharged V8 petrol engines was to reduce the differences between the Jaguar and Land Rover variants of the engine.

The existing situation was admittedly rather complex. Jaguar's AJ-V8 engine had been introduced in 1996 with a 4.0-litre capacity, and had gone through various iterations in the ensuing years. There was even a special 3.9-litre version between 2000 and 2005, built only in the USA and used for a series of Lincoln and Ford models – and there were special Aston Martin-assembled versions, too. However, at the time when the engine had entered the Range Rover Sport story, the primary Jaguar version had a swept volume of 4.2 litres and could be had as a naturally aspirated (AJ33) engine with 294bhp, or a supercharged (AJ33S) type with 390bhp.

As explained in Chapter 2, Land Rover happily took on the supercharged 4.2-litre engine for the Sport, but needed a specially designed 4.4-litre version as well to replace the 4.4-litre BMW V8 in the Range Rover. Jaguar knew this as

This was another of the remarkable cutaways produced for the 2010 model-year, showing the layout of the new 5.0-litre V8.

For petrol-oriented markets, the big news for 2010 was the new 5.0-litre LR-V8 engine.

the AJ41 engine, but it was only ever built for Land Rover. The plan for 2010 was to reduce production complication by developing a new version of the engine that would have a single swept volume to suit both naturally aspirated and supercharged engines, and to suit both Jaguar and Land Rover applications. The programme to develop that engine settled on a 5.0-litre capacity. For Jaguar cars, the new 5.0-litre V8 was known as an AJ133 type; for Land Rover products, the engine was called the LR-V8. Both had to conform to the upcoming EU5 emissions regulations in Europe, and to the ULEV2 regulations in the USA.

The basic architecture of the 5.0-litre engines was the same as that of earlier JLR V8s, with four camshafts and 4 valves per cylinder. However, a huge amount of redevelopment went into them. The block was completely redesigned, with bigger bores and a longer stroke to give the extra capacity. The

The supercharged V8 also went to a 5.0-litre size for 2010.

The exhaust manifolds of the supercharged V8 were not, of course, chromed like those on the demonstration model!

As this cutaway shows, the supercharger was actually mounted in the V at the back of the engine.

fuelling system was also new, and depended on spray-guided direct fuel injection, the first of its kind in the industry.

The primary aims of the redesign were class-leading economy and improved low-end torque. A new cooling system that allowed faster warm-up made its contribution to better economy, as did a lower idling speed and a number of low-friction design features. More obviously, both inlet and exhaust camshafts featured continuously variable timing. For the naturally aspirated V8s there was also cam profile switching and a variable-length inlet manifold, while the supercharged versions had a sixth-generation Eaton twin-vortex supercharger and an intercooler. To control these massively complicated engines, the engine designers chose a Denso Generation 1.6 management system.

The improvements were impressive enough on paper, and even more so on the road. As built for the Range Rover Sport, the naturally aspirated 5.0-litre V8 delivered 375bhp, up by 25 per cent from the 300bhp of the earlier 4.4-litre engine. The supercharged 5.0-litre engine had a huge 510bhp, up by 31 per cent from the 390bhp of the 4.2-litre supercharged type. It also posted improvements in both fuel economy (reduced by 6.2 per cent overall) and CO_2 levels (reduced by 5.6 per cent).

Inevitably there were some differences between the Jaguar and Land Rover versions of these engines. The Land Rover versions had deeper sumps to cope with different lubrication demands, and they also had additional waterproofing. The belt drives, alternator, air-conditioning compressor, PAS pump and starter motor were all specially waterproofed to protect them in wading situations, which of course were not expected to occur with the Jaguar versions.

Both naturally aspirated and supercharged 5.0-litre V8 engines were made for JLR by Ford in the Bridgend factory, where the earlier petrol V8s had also been manufactured.

CHASSIS CHANGES

The new and more powerful engines were just the start of the 2010 changes, which also included a number of chassis refinements to emphasize the model's sporting character. Stiffer front suspension bushes gave better steering response, while the Supercharged model went to unique new Brembo six-piston front-brake callipers on ventilated discs, and the TDV8 diesel took on the four-piston Brembo set-up from the outgoing supercharged car. Both models had ventilated rear discs with lightweight aluminium, single-piston callipers, but the discs on the Supercharged car were larger. Land Rover claimed a better pedal feel, too.

Completely new was Adaptive Dynamics, a system that was integrated with the existing Dynamic Response suspension to ensure that a refined ride and sharp handling were no longer mutually exclusive. On Supercharged models it was called 'active roll control'. Central to the system were new DampTronic dampers, made by Bilstein but actually developed in-house by Land Rover, which incorporated continuously adjustable valves. Damper pressure on each wheel was monitored 500 times a second, and predictive technology enabled the system to be prepared for the road ahead, rather than having to react to it.

The new DampTronic dampers had continuously adjustable valves.

The new sixth setting for the Terrain Response was indicated by a winding motorway symbol, and optimized the vehicle's systems for fast cruising.

There were multiple changes to the dynamic control systems, too. A refinement to the stability control system helped to slow the vehicle automatically on a bend taken too fast, while the off-road Hill Descent Control took on a new gradient release control, which prevented a sudden lurch as the vehicle's brakes were released on a steep downhill slope.

On top of that, Terrain Response was extensively revised, gaining a new sixth setting that was unique to the Sport. Known as Dynamic (and actually previewed on the Terrain Response control of the Range Stormer concept car back in 2004), this setting made adjustments to the adaptive dynamics system, stiffening the rear anti-roll setting by 20 per cent, and altering the accelerator pedal mapping and the gearchange settings to give a more sporty drive. The sand and rock crawl settings were also revised; the sand stetting now incorporated sand launch control to limit wheel slip on initial driveaway and to reduce the chance of the wheels digging into soft sand, while the rock crawl settings now gave finer control.

EXTERIOR CHANGES

Even though the Sport had been the most successful of Land Rover's products, customer feedback suggested that it needed to be given a more distinct identity. So the changes for 2010 added sophistication and sporting flavour, but retained the Range Rover brand characteristic of restraint. The visual changes that gave the 2010 Sport its distinctive character were developed by a team working under new design chief Gerry McGovern, who had taken over from Geoff Upex when the latter retired in 2006. Overall, they gave the model a more sporting and aerodynamic stance.

Several factors influenced this reworking of the original Richard Woolley design. Prominent among them was Land Rover's belief that reducing the apparent size of its vehicles would deflect criticism at a time when large vehicles had become seen in some quarters as politically incorrect purchases. So the front end was redesigned with a larger apron air intake and a slimming two-element grille that also helped to distinguish the Sport from the Range Rover with its new three-element grille.

At the same time, customer approval of the Stormer bodykit with its heavily sculpted look had suggested a way forward,

ABOVE: **This 2010 model on display at the Canary Wharf MotorExpo showcased the new Bali Blue paint option.**

The 2010 models were easy to recognize from the side by the twin-stripe motif on their air vents. This one also has the new Style 6 20in alloy wheels.

and the front and rear bumper aprons were redesigned in that idiom; the front wings had to be altered as well, to accommodate this new look. With the new front wings came new side vents that incorporated twin horizontal highlight strips, matching the twin elements of the new grille and the twin horizontal stripes of the new front and rear indicator lights.

Those redesigned lights added to the new appearance. The headlamp units still incorporated the intersecting circles from the original design, but there were now pinpoint LED lights around the main light units, which were designed to meet forthcoming new European regulations that required all vehicles to have daytime running lights. They were certainly distinctive – Land Rover publicity material described them as 'signature' lights, meaning that their distinctive shape was immediately identifiable as belonging to a Range Rover Sport – but this initial design did not go down very well with the buyers. Some thought it was rather too dainty and too easily compared to the lights on a Christmas tree.

The new rear-lamp units not only incorporated the twin-stripe motif for their indicator segments, but also had a bolder appearance than before. There was a deliberate resemblance to their equivalents on the latest Range Rover, which also had a makeover for 2010. Also new at the rear was a body-coloured plinth for the Range Rover name, which contributed to the overall cleaner appearance of the new models.

There were, of course, changes to the colour palette and to the alloy wheel options for 2010. The new colours added some brightness to the options list, while there were now seven different wheel styles for the Sport range, rather unimaginatively named Style 1 to Style 7. The smallest standard wheels now had a 19in diameter (an inch up on the 2009 range), and no fewer than five of the seven options had a 20in diameter. Probably most eye-catching was a new 20in style with five spokes that resembled scimitar blades, and Land Rover featured these heavily in publicity photographs when the new models were announced in summer 2009.

ABOVE LEFT: **The twin-stripe motif was carried through into the tail-lights of the 2010 models, where the horizontal lights were used as turn indicators.**

ABOVE MIDDLE: **The daytime running lights on the 2010 models were certainly distinctive, but were not to everyone's taste.**

ABOVE RIGHT: **Style 7 wheels had diamond-turned highlights contrasting with an otherwise dark finish, but were otherwise the same as the Style 6 option.**

The 2010 Range Rover Sports were the last ones with Land Rover branding on their wheel centre caps.

BELOW LEFT: **The two 19in wheel options for 2010: Style 1 at the top and Style 5 below.**

BELOW RIGHT: **Clockwise from the top, these 20in wheel options are Style 3, Style 4, Style 7 and Style 6.**

19 INCH 5 V-SPOKE ALLOYS
'STYLE 1'

19 INCH 15-SPOKE ALLOYS
'STYLE 5'

20 INCH 15-SPOKE ALLOYS
'STYLE 3'

20 INCH 15-SPOKE ALLOYS
DIAMOND TURNED FINISH 'STYLE 4'

20 INCH 5-SPOKE ALLOYS
'STYLE 6'

20 INCH 5-SPOKE ALLOYS
DIAMOND TURNED FINISH 'STYLE 7'

GERRY MCGOVERN

Gerry McGovern became Chief Styling Officer for the Land Rover side of JLR.

Design Director Gerry McGovern became the highly recognizable 'talking head' of Land Rover in the later 2000s, and remained so as this book was being prepared. While still at school in Coventry he was sponsored by Roy Axe, then Design Director for Chrysler, to do a degree in industrial design. He then went to the Royal College of Art in London to study automotive design.

McGovern spent some time working for Chrysler in Detroit before returning to the UK to work for the company's Peugeot division in the Midlands. In 1982 he rejoined Roy Axe, who had become Design Director of what was by then called Austin Rover. In the 1980s he worked on the MG EX-E concept car, moving on to lead design on the MGF sports car released in 1995, and then switching to the Land Rover side of the house where he led the team that designed the 1997 Freelander.

Head-hunted by Ford (who did not at that stage own Land Rover), McGovern went to America in 1999 to revitalize design for that company's Lincoln and Mercury brands. He returned to the UK in 2003 to run Ford's London-based design centre, and then in 2004 rejoined Land Rover as Director, Advanced Design, under Geoff Upex. Two years later he took over from Upex as the head of Land Rover Design.

His first major new design for the company was the LRX concept car in 2007, which went on to become the Range Rover Evoque that was launched in 2011, and also set a distinctive new design direction for Land Rover models.

INTERIOR REVISIONS

The changes inside the 2010-model Sport's passenger cabin were, if anything, even more comprehensive than those for the exterior. They were largely driven, according to Gerry McGovern, by customer requests for the interior to be 'more Range Rover'.

So the 2010 models were given the full luxury treatment, with higher quality materials and soft-touch finishes to create what Land Rover described as a 'premium environment'. The basic 'cockpit' design with its high centre console was retained, but there was much more leather throughout, with a new and wider choice of colours. A new steering wheel incorporated a pair of five-way 'joysticks' to control the

infotainment systems and the new driver information screen in the instrument pack, and it could be fitted with paddle switches for rapid gear changing, a feature borrowed from high-performance cars and one that reinforced the model's sporting ambience. Meanwhile, the Sport retained its unique character, with new seats front and rear that were more shape-hugging than before, and electrically adjustable side bolsters on the options list.

The facia had been considerably cleaned up, with 50 per cent fewer switches, and many functions were now accessed through the touch-screen in the centre of the dash. The switches that did remain had a chrome-plated finish. There was a new instrument pack, shared with the Discovery 4, where the main instrument dials were much less cluttered

Still featuring the 'cockpit' feel of the original, the driver's environment of the 2010 models had cleaner lines and felt more luxurious than before.

The new TFT screen between the main dials is configured here to show engine temperature and fuel-tank contents. The panel at the top allows the cruise control to be set to maintain a set gap from the vehicle ahead, and the previous journey supposedly achieved a remarkable average of 8.8ltr/100km (32mpg). Clearly, this one was a diesel!

than before. Between them was a 12cm (5in) driver information screen (incorporating 'thin film technology'), which delivered key information very effectively and replaced the earlier message centre screen.

A new portable audio interface allowed USB sticks, iPODs and the like to be hooked up to the car's ICE system and controlled from the touch screen. Particularly welcome was the new analogue clock that replaced the barely legible digital read-out on the centre console of the earlier Sports. Then there was a new ambient lighting system with white LEDs that cast subtle halos around the interior door handles and pockets, as well as on the facia and the centre console area.

Several of the features new to the 2010 Sport were shared with other models in the range. A remote fob allowed both keyless entry and a keyless start when receivers in the vehicle sensed its proximity, while High Beam Assist in the new LED headlights both switched the lights on when the ambient light fell below a certain threshold, and dipped the headlights automatically when it detected the lights of an oncoming vehicle. The latest hard-drive navigation system was fitted.

Tow Assist made hitching up to a trailer easier by displaying the view to the rear of the vehicle on to the dashboard touch-screen with an overlay of guidance lines, and there were five cameras in the Surround Camera System, which made low-speed manoeuvring easier with a clear on-screen view of the area immediately around the vehicle.

... AND THE REST

Even this extensive list of changes did not tell the full story of the 2010 Range Rover Sport. Land Rover also

THE MEN AT THE TOP

Land Rover and Jaguar had been part of Ford's Premium Automotive Group, but after a shake-up in mid-2005 they were integrated as Jaguar Land Rover. Both administrative and manufacturing operations were to be integrated, and in September that year Geoff Polites was made their Chief Executive Officer with the brief of returning them to profit. Polites was a highly respected and long-serving executive who had spent a forty-year career with Ford, and he successfully returned the combined marques to profit, so enabling Ford to put them up for sale in 2008.

By this stage, Polites was suffering from cancer, and he did not live to see the sale completed. He died in late April 2008, and Financial Director David Smith was given the job of seeing the deal through in June. Smith was then formally appointed as JLR's new CEO. However, he did not stay in the job for long, and resigned in January 2010 for reasons that were not made public at the time.

JLR director Ravi Kant, a Tata appointee, now became caretaker CEO until a permanent appointee was found: that was Dr Ralf Speth, who took the job in February 2010. Bavarian-born Speth had worked for BMW for twenty years before spending some time with the Linde Group, and then becoming the Premium Automotive Group's Director of Production, Quality and Planning in 2007. Much liked within JLR, Speth also became a Non-Executive Director of Tata Motors in November 2010.

ABOVE: **Dr Ralf Speth took over as CEO of JLR in 2010.**

LEFT: **David Smith became JLR's new CEO in 2008, and oversaw the sale to Tata.**

incorporated some of its new 'environmental' technologies in the new models, notable among them being an 'intelligent power management system' that included 'smart regenerative charging'. The alternator charged the battery when the vehicle was coasting but not when it was accelerating, so reducing drag on the engine and therefore fuel consumption. Drag on the engine was also reduced by the clutch on the new air-conditioning pump, which now disengaged when the air conditioning was off.

Right across the board, the 2010 models also shared a new and stronger six-speed automatic gearbox, known as the 6HP28 type. It was a straightforward development of the earlier 6HP26 type, and was, of course, again manufactured by ZF in Germany. The 6HP28 incorporated an intelligent Sport mode that could adapt to different driving styles. It also contributed to fuel economy through earlier torque converter lock-up, which in turn was made feasible by the higher torque of the new engines. And for the sporting driver, those optional paddle shifts on the steering wheel gave effortless manual control of gearchanges.

COLOUR AND TRIM OPTIONS, 2010 MODELS

There were fourteen paint options during the 2010 model-year, although only thirteen were available at any one time, and there was a substitution in January 2010. Bali Blue, Ipanema Sand, Marmaris Teal and Nara Bronze were all new. Four colours were not carried over from 2009: these were Atacama Sand, Cairns Blue and Lucerne Green, while Lugano Teal disappeared at the end of 2009. All these paints were metallic types except for Alaska White, which was a traditional 'solid' type.

There were now three styles of upholstery: leather, Premium leather (which now had perforated wearing surfaces), and leather with Alcantara wearing surfaces. Colour availability was as follows:

Standard leather:	Almond, Ebony, Ocean
Premium leather:	Almond, Arabica, Ebony, Ivory, Tan
Leather with Alcantara:	Almond/Nutmeg, Ebony/Lunar, Ivory/Ocean, Ivory/Lunar

There was an optional extended leather pack, which added leather to the four door armrests and top rolls, the dash-board top, the instrument panel peak and the end caps of the dashboard. The dashboard top was finished either in Ebony, or to match the seat upholstery.

When Ebony Premium leather was ordered with contrast stitching, the Lunar stitch normally used on the door armrests and cubby box was replaced by Ebony stitch.

There were also three varieties of wood trim panel: Anigre (gloss), Grand Black Lacquer (gloss) and Straight Grain Walnut (with a satin finish). These options made for a complex set of interior options, which were grouped into six 'colourways'. These were as follows:

Almond/Nutmeg:	Almond seats with Nutmeg carpet; or Almond and Nutmeg seats with Nutmeg carpet. Straight Grain Walnut wood was the designer's choice.
Arabica/Almond:	Arabica seats with Nutmeg carpet. Anigre wood was the designer's choice.
Ebony:	Ebony seats with Ebony carpet; or Ebony and Lunar seats with Ebony carpet. Grand Black Lacquer wood was the designer's choice.
Ebony/Ivory:	Ivory seats with Ebony carpet; or Ivory and Lunar seats with Ebony carpet. Grand Black Lacquer wood was the designer's choice.
Ebony/Tan:	Tan seats with Ebony carpet. Grand Black Lacquer wood was the designer's choice.
Ocean/Ivory:	Ocean seats with Ocean carpet; or Ivory seats with Ocean carpet; or Ivory and Ocean seats with Ocean carpet. Anigre wood was the designer's choice.

Most combinations were feasible, although Land Rover did refuse to provide some combinations that they considered did not work; in sales catalogues they also highlighted the ones they thought worked best by describing them as 'designer's choice' options.

COLOUR AND TRIM OPTIONS

Paint	Codes	Notes
Alaska White	909, NCL	Designer's choices were Ivory seats with Ocean carpet, and Ivory and Ocean seats with Ocean carpet
Bali Blue	823, JBL	Not available with Arabica/Almond, Almond/Nutmeg or Ebony/Tan colourways. Designer's choice was the Ebony colourway
Bournville	822, AAD	Not available with Ocean/Ivory colourway. Designer's choice was the Arabica/Almond colourway
Buckingham Blue	796, JGJ	Designer's choice was the Ebony/Ivory colourway
Galway Green	821, HAC	Designer's choice was the Almond/Nutmeg colourway
Ipanema Sand	824, GAQ	Designer's choice was the Ebony/Ivory colourway
Izmir Blue	920, MWE	Designer's choice was the Ebony colourway
Lugano Teal	963, JMB	Available until end 2009 only. Designer's choices were Ivory seats with Ocean carpet, and Ivory and Ocean seats with Ocean carpet
Marmaris Teal	826, JCK	Replaced Lugano Teal in January 2010. Designer's choices were Ivory seats with Ocean carpet, and Ivory and Ocean seats with Ocean carpet
Nara Bronze	825, AAJ	Designer's choice was the Arabica/Almond colourway
Rimini Red	889, CBK	Not available with Ocean/Ivory colourway. Designer's choice was the Almond/Nutmeg colourway
Santorini Black	820, PAB	Designer's choices were the Ebony/Ivory and Ebony/Tan colourways
Stornoway Grey	907, LEL	Designer's choice was the Ebony colourway
Zermatt Silver	798, MBK	Designer's choices were Ocean seats with Ocean carpets, and the Ebony/Tan colourway

WHEEL AND TYRE OPTIONS, 2010 MODEL-YEAR

Specification	Style	Description
SE	Style 1	19in × 9J with five V-spokes, Sparkle Silver finish and 255/50R19 tyres
HSE	Style 2	20in × 9.5J Stormer with nine spokes, Titan Silver finish and 275/40R20 tyres
	Style 3	20in × 9.5J fifteen-spoke with Sparkle Silver finish and 275/40R20 tyres
	Style 4	20in × 9.5J fifteen-spoke with diamond-turned finish and 275/40R20 tyres
	Style 5	19in × 9J fifteen-spoke with 255/50R19 tyres
Supercharged	Style 6	20in × 9.5J five-spoke with 275/40R20 tyres
	Style 7	20in × 9.5J five-spoke with diamond-turned finish and 275/40R20 tyres
Autobiography	Style 8	20in × 9.5J ten-spoke with diamond-turned finish and 275/40R20 tyres

WHAT THE PRESS THOUGHT

The 2010-model Range Rover Sport was introduced at the London MotorExpo held at Canary Wharf on 8 June 2009. Media representatives were soon given the opportunity to try examples, and generally reacted very favourably. *Autocar* magazine reported in its issue of 12 August:

> There's a certain arrogance about the Range Rover Sport, but it has much to be arrogant about. The overall aim, Land Rover says, is to make the car 'More sporty and more sophisticated'. Aside from some of the more crass stylistic details, the company has achieved its aim.

However, writer Hilton Holloway definitely did not like some of the new design features: 'We could live without the blingy exterior details… an aesthetically toned-down version would be welcome.' Nevertheless, there was no denying the improvements in handling:

> Usually the side forces that build up when the driver accelerates around a bend result in a counter reaction of body roll when the car straightens up – but not here. There's an uncanny delicacy in the way the chassis electronics can gather the Sport's tall body and marshal the shifting weight when it is driven briskly on winding B roads. The new, variable-ratio steering also has a new-found accuracy, biting immediately off the straight-ahead, making it easy to place the car on the narrowest of roads.

Car magazine tested a TDV6 model that August, and came away impressed: 'It looks sharper and sleeker, is much nicer inside, and is better to drive. It's all the car you'll ever need.'

The new engine came in for particular praise from writer Ben Pullman:

> Cleaner, more economical and yet more powerful, the new 3.0-litre diesel addresses all the shortcomings of the old 2.7-litre. The engine is smoother and more refined across the entire rev range, so there's not a constant agricultural racket accompanying you wherever you go. It cruises quietly and serenely at 80mph, with only a slight whistle from big door mirrors.

The main criticism concerned interior space:

> The only downside is that the Range Sport still isn't huge. There's space for five inside, but the upright dash architecture eats into front passenger knee room – and there's two tiny gloveboxes rather than a single large one – and rear seat and boot space is only adequate.

WHEEL AND TYRE OPTIONS, 2010 MODEL-YEAR

Centre caps normally carried a gold-on-green Land Rover logo, but those for the Supercharged models were silver on black.

RANGE ROVER SPORT SPECIAL EDITIONS

The Range Rover Sport Autobiography

As the market gradually recovered from the doldrums of 2009, so Land Rover decided to give it a boost with a special edition Sport at the top of the price range. So the first quarter of 2010 saw the arrival of the 500-strong Range Rover Autobiography edition. Announced in January, it became available through showrooms in March.

Land Rover had first used the Autobiography name to describe its bespoke customization service for Range Rovers back in 1993. However, the name increasingly became used for limited edition models as well, and by 2010 it was

no great surprise to see it used this way on the Range Rover Sport. The Sport Autobiography came only with the supercharged or TDV8 engines, and it pioneered a new bodykit of bumpers, rear spoiler and exhaust finishers that had been designed to suit the revised lines of the 2010 models.

The grille and side vents both had a special Titan finish, and the mirror caps were painted in the body colour. On super-

The new Autobiography Sport was introduced part-way through the 2010 model-year as a special edition, and was readily recognizable by its bodykit. This was one of the preview pictures issued to the media in September 2009.

At the rear, the Autobiography Sport had a longer spoiler above the rear window, and a different apron incorporating rectangular exhaust outlets.

The Autobiography Sport came with two special interior options, both with the Autobiography name moulded into the head restraints. This was the Monaco colourway with Ebony and Ivory upholstery...

... and this striking combination of Pimento and Ebony, known as the Monza colourway.

charged versions only there were also approach lamps in the door mirrors, shining a light on the ground beside the vehicle when the central locking had been remotely unlocked. The latest Style 8 diamond-turned 20in wheels were standard wear, and inevitably there was a special Autobiography badge on the tailgate.

There was a degree of drama about the passenger cabin, which could be had with a choice of two duo-tone finishes. The Monaco colourway brought a combination of Ebony and Ivory Premium leather, and even more striking was the Monza colourway that combined Pimento with Ebony. Steering wheels (with paddle shifts, of course) were two-toned to match, the head restraints were embossed with the Autobiography logo, and there were even special sill tread plates. The wood trim with both options was Grand Black Lacquer, also with an Autobiography logo on each front door, and the extended leather option was standard. Then there was a cooler in the centre console; DSC and Trailer Stability Assist were both standard; and to top it all off, these models were

supplied with a specially covered driver's handbook and key chain fob.

The Range Rover Sport Ultimate

There was also a special edition of the Range Rover Sport for the French market in 2010. Based on the TDV8 model and released in April 2010, the Range Rover Sport Ultimate was an eighty-strong edition priced between the HSE and the French HSE Premium models.

The Ultimate came with a choice of two different 20in alloy wheel styles, with the Adaptive Dynamics chassis package, and with the Bi-Xenon front lighting system. The interior featured extended leather with Grand Black Lacquer wood, and a heated windscreen, heated seats and heated steering wheel rim were all standard. The steering wheel had paddle shifts, the centre console contained a coolbox, and there was Premium carpet all round.

Technical Specifications, 2010

Engines

(1) 3.0-litre TDV6 diesel
2993cc (84 × 90mm) Ford-Peugeot ohv V6 diesel with 4 valves
    per cylinder, common-rail injection, twin parallel sequential
    turbochargers and intercooler (EU5 compliant)
Bosch Gen 3 engine-management system
16:1 compression ratio
245bhp at 4,000rpm
442lb/ft at 2,000rpm

(2) 3.6-litre TDV8 diesel
3630cc (81 × 88mm) Ford-Land Rover ohv V8 diesel
    with 4 valves per cylinder, common-rail injection, twin
    turbochargers and intercooler
17.3:1 compression ratio
268bhp at 4,000rpm
472lb/ft at 2,000rpm

(3) 5-litre V8 petrol
5000cc (92.5 × 93mm) Jaguar-Land Rover LR-V8 petrol V8
    with four camshafts and 4 valves per cylinder
9.5:1 compression ratio
375bhp at 6,000rpm
375lb/ft at 2,500rpm

(4) 5-litre supercharged V8 petrol
5000cc (92.5 × 93mm) Jaguar-Land Rover LR-V8 petrol V8
    with four camshafts and 4 valves per cylinder plus Eaton
    twin-vortex supercharger and intercooler
9.5:1 compression ratio
510bhp at 6,000rpm
460lb/ft at 2,500rpm

Transmission
Permanent four-wheel drive with centre differential
    incorporating viscous coupling to give automatic locking;
    Terrain Response traction system standard; optional locking
    rear differential

Final drive ratio: 3.73:1 (V8 petrol models)
                        3.54:1 (TDV6, TDV8 and V8 Supercharged
                        models)

Primary gearbox:
Six-speed ZF 6HP28 automatic; ratios 4.171:1, 2.340:1,
    1.521:1, 1.143:1, 0.867:1, 0.691:1, reverse 3.403:1

Transfer gearbox:
Separate two-speed type with 'active' centre differential; high
    ratio 1:1, low ratio 2.93:1

Suspension
Independent front and rear suspension with height-adjustable
electronic air suspension and telescopic dampers; double
wishbones front and rear

Steering
ZF Servotronic speed proportional power-assisted rack and
pinion

Brakes
Four-wheel disc brakes with dual hydraulic line, servo
assistance and Bosch four-channel ABS
Ventilated front discs with 360mm diameter and twin-piston
sliding callipers (TDV6 and TDV8, 2010), or 380mm
diameter with six-piston fixed callipers (supercharged V8)
Ventilated rear discs with 350mm diameter and single-piston
sliding callipers (TDV6 and TDV8) or 365mm diameter with
single-piston sliding callipers (supercharged V8)
Servo-operated parking brake operating on drums within the
rear discs

Vehicle dimensions

Wheelbase:	2,745mm (108.1in)
Overall length:	4,788mm (188.5in)
Overall width:	1,928mm (75.9in); 2,170mm (85.4in) over mirrors

Overall height:	1,817mm (71.5in) at standard ride height
Unladen weight (for typical UK-market models):	(1) 3.6-litre TDV8 models: 2,656–2,756kg (5,855–6,076lb)
	(2) 3.0-litre TDV6 models: 2,535–2,670kg (5,588–5,886lb)
	(3) 5.0-litre supercharged V8 models: 2,590–2,679kg (5,710–5,906lb)

Performance

(1) 3.0-litre TDV6 models

Max. speed:	193km/h (120mph)
0–60mph:	8.8sec

(2) 3.6-litre TDV8 models

Max. speed:	210km/h (130mph)
0–60mph:	8.6sec

(3) 5.0-litre petrol V8 models

Max. speed:	210km/h (130mph)
0–60mph:	7.2sec

(4) 5.0-litre V8 supercharged models

Max. speed:	225km/h (140mph)
0–60mph:	5.9sec

CHAPTER SIX

THE FINAL MODELS, 2011–2013

Only very close observers of Land Rover and its products would have realized that a replacement for the L320 Range Rover Sport could not have been far off after the 2010 model-year facelift. Work had certainly begun on project L494, which was to deliver a second-generation Sport and would be made public in March 2013. That very same month was to be the last one for production of L320.

Nevertheless, the final two and a half years of L320 production brought multiple changes to the model, keeping it cosmetically fresh and also enabling it to meet the new European EU5 exhaust emissions regulations that became law from the start of 2011. Meanwhile, Land Rover gradually moved the Sport more and more upmarket, until it was closer in nature to the full-size Range Rover, thus making it more of a 'premium' product (in the public relations language of the day). Inevitably, prices increased: in the first quarter of 2010, a Supercharged Autobiography Sport cost £69,995; by the time production ended in 2013, that same model was priced at £76,330.

This was also a period when Land Rover previewed the hybrid powertrains that they had promised at the time of the Land_e concept displayed at the Geneva Show in February 2006. Although no hybrid version of L320 was ever intended to go into production, an early version of the system planned for L494 was made public on a series of special L320 development vehicles, of which the first was shown at Geneva in March 2011. Deliberately harking back to the earlier (non-running) concept, these were known as Range_e models (see section below).

Land Rover announced its diesel hybrid Range_e in May 2010, and issued this publicity picture. Sharp eyes will spot that it is a left-hand-drive vehicle and that the side graphics differ from those seen on later Range_e models. So was it real, or was it just an ordinary Sport mocked up for some advance publicity?

Three views of three different vehicles show the way the Sport looked for the 2011 model-year.

Sales of the L320 Sport held up very well in these final two and a half years of production. The 2011 calendar year saw production bounce back up to 58,459, which was a handful above the figure for L320's second-best year of 2006. This improvement was undoubtedly directly attributable to the 2010 facelift models, and to the further enhanced specifications for the 2011 model-year, although it was also true that the global economy was recovering after the doldrums of 2009, and that car sales in general were picking up again.

Land Rover more or less repeated the trick in 2012, when calendar-year production was only around 600 lower than for 2011. And the figures for the three months in which L320 was built in 2013 suggested that there would have been no slowdown had production continued for the full twelve months. So the Sport brand was on a high when the new L494 models were introduced to replace the original model.

THE 2011 MODELS: AN ENLARGED TDV8

For Land Rover as a company, the big news at the start of the 2011 model-year was the introduction of the new Range Rover Evoque at the Paris Motor Show in September. Changes for the other ranges were minimized in order to ensure that the focus remained on the newcomer, but there were nonetheless some important adjustments to the Range Rover Sport line-up.

As before, there was a range of four engines. British buyers were offered just two of them – the 245bhp TDV6, which was available in the SE, HSE and Autobiography models, and the 510bhp supercharged V8, which came with either HSE or Autobiography equipment levels. For export, however, there remained the 5.0-litre naturally aspirated petrol V8 with 375bhp, and there was also the option of a newly enlarged TDV8.

Extensively redeveloped, in plenty of time to meet the Euro 5 emissions regulations that would come into force in January 2011, the new TDV8 had a swept volume of 4.4 litres. Both bore and stroke had been enlarged, and the twin turbocharger installation was now a parallel sequential type similar in principle to that on the 3.0-litre TDV6. With its 308bhp, this engine developed huge maximum torque of 516lb/ft, which completely eclipsed any other engine then available in the Sport. CO_2 emissions were down by 14 per cent as compared with the 3.6-litre engine that it replaced (to 253g/km), and there was even an improvement in fuel consumption. The 4.4-litre TDV8 became the only diesel option for the full-size Range Rover, but Land Rover judged that Britain would prefer a further developed TDV6 that was on the horizon for summer 2011, and as a result there were no examples of the new engine in Range Rover Sports sold on Solihull's home market.

The major news for 2011 was the new 4.4-litre TDV8, although it was not made available in Britain. This one is in a car for the German market, and was pictured in the Solihull plant in April 2010, some time before the official announcement.

The sales brochures remained bright and cheerful for the 2011 model-year.

British buyers were, of course, offered the other novelties introduced for the 2011 season. These included an optional dark finish called Jupiter for the radiator grille, and the availability as an accessory of the new bodykit seen on the summer-special Autobiography, complete with black vents and black honeycomb grille. This was now called the

Enhanced Design Pack. Paint options had their annual adjustment, but the interior options remained unchanged except for the Autobiography models. The range of equipment levels remained the same as for 2010, the entry-level models being SE types; HSE was now the mid-range level, and above that came the Autobiography. Following its successful debut over the summer of 2010 in limited-edition form, this now became a full production option – and with some changes.

Whereas the limited-edition Autobiography had come with either the TDV8 or the supercharged engine, in Britain the full production models for 2011 offered a choice between the TDV6 diesel and the Supercharged V8. They could be had with only six of the thirteen exterior colour options: these were Bali Blue, Fuji White, Nara Bronze, Santorini Black, Stornoway Grey and Zermatt Silver. There was a wider choice for the interior, however, as the Monaco and Monza options of the limited edition were joined by Le Mans, with seats in Ebony and Tan. Grand Black Lacquer was once again the standard wood trim, and upholstery was in Premium perforated leather with contrast stitching as standard.

The next major event affecting the Sport during the 2011 model-year came in March 2011, when a Range Rover Sport with hybrid diesel-electric powertrain was

The accessory bodykit was rather grandly described in sales literature as an enhanced design pack – which admittedly sounded rather more sophisticated. Here it is on a 2011 model with Autobiography diamond-turned 20in wheels.

The Sport's basic strengths were not lost amid all the design changes. In September 2010, the Caravan Club voted it 'Towcar of the Year' in its class.

BELOW LEFT: The special tailgate badge on Autobiography models had the three-dimensional, cast style seen on other contemporary Land Rover vehicle badges.

BELOW RIGHT: This was the special grille used on Autobiography models...

... and this was the special style of side vents, carrying Range Rover branding.

There were special kick panels for the Autobiography Sport, too.

announced at the Geneva Show in March 2011 – although the awkwardly named Range_e (see below) was a development model that was not intended to enter production. Meanwhile, far away in Japan, a major earthquake and consequent tsunami struck on 11 March, with a devastating effect on the country and its people. One casualty was the factory at Onahama owned by German paint manufacturer

Merck, where operations were suspended immediately. As this was the only factory in the world to manufacture a pigment called Xirallic (an aluminium-oxide-crystal compound) that created a pearlescent sparkle, car makers world-wide found themselves unable to obtain supplies of paint that depended on it.

Although the factory reopened in May and Merck claimed to have caught up on back orders by the beginning of September, there was considerable disruption over the summer. Land Rover had no choice but to suspend supplies of six colours used on the Range Rover Sport (see the table Colours and Trims below), although as a temporary expedient it introduced two new colours that were similar to two of those affected. Orkney Grey was planned for the 2012 model-year and reappeared then, but Sumatra Black was unique to this period of difficulty in 2011 and therefore remains a rare colour on the Range Rover Sport.

The Range_e Hybrid Prototype

The Range_e hybrid prototype shown at Geneva in March 2011 was part of an ultra low-carbon fleet trial that was sponsored by the UK government's Technology Strategy Board. By the time it was made public, Jaguar Land Rover had a team of 139 engineers working on hybrid powertrains, led by Peter Richards as Chief Engineer, Hybrids. A number of charging points had also been installed at various JLR sites to assist evaluation of the technology in real-world use.

The Range_e was never intended to be a production car, but was a development vehicle that prototyped and evaluated a hybrid electric-diesel powertrain. JLR claimed that such a powertrain would become available in production models during 2013, and the second-generation Range Rover Sport was indeed made available with such a system.

The powertrain in the Range_e combined a 245PS TDV6 diesel engine with a 69kW electric motor to create a parallel hybrid system. This meant that the vehicle could be driven on electric power alone, on diesel power alone, or with both power systems in use, when a total power output of 339PS was available. An intelligent system on the vehicle determined the most efficient way of delivering the power required, as determined by the use of the accelerator pedal. The whole powertrain drove through an eight-speed ZF gearbox, which by March 2011 was not yet available in the L320 Sport – but soon would be.

The TFT screen on the instrument panel of the Sport is displaying fuel and temperature information here, but it could be reconfigured to give a variety of other information of use to the driver.

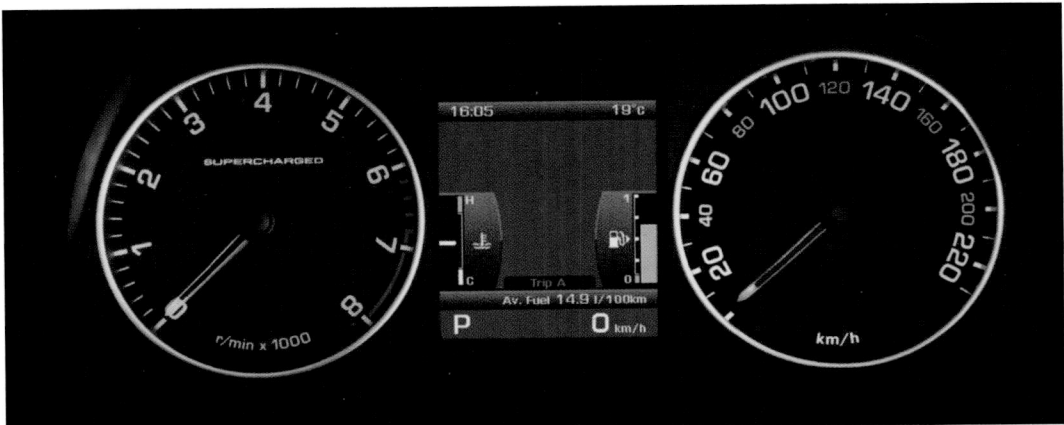

Definitely the real thing! This was one of the Range_e hybrid prototypes that was used for testing. It is seen plugged into a recharging point. Note that the twin fillers – one for diesel and one for electricity – are on the opposite side to the standard fuel filler.

Emissions were the main focus of the Range_e experimental vehicles, and this point was displayed prominently on each one.

The Range_e was part of Land Rover's E-terrain Technologies programme.

Electric power was provided from a 14.2kW/h lithium-ion battery mounted on the vehicle. This could be recharged from an external 240-volt power source (which would take around four hours from a typical domestic supply). The Range_e also had a regenerative braking system to convert the energy normally dissipated from the brakes as heat into electricity to charge the battery. On electric power alone, the Range_e would provide 32km (20 miles) of emissions-free motoring at speeds up to 113km/h (70mph). The Land Rover press release read:

Typically, the majority of European car drivers cover less than 40km (25 miles) a day, and therefore the EV range offered by this technology will support the majority of short urban journeys, where fuel economy and emissions are of prime concern.

For longer journeys, the diesel engine engaged and the hybrid powertrain continually optimized CO_2 emissions, delivering a maximum speed of around 190km/h (120mph). Land Rover claimed fuel economy of up to 3.3ltr/100km (85mpg) and a range of 1,110km (690 miles) on a full tank of diesel. The CO_2 rating of the Range_e was 89g/km, as compared to 243g/km for a standard TDV6-powered Sport.

Over the summer of 2011, five Range_e prototypes entered a test programme with other manufacturers who belonged to the CABLED (Coventry and Birmingham Low Emissions Demonstrators) consortium.

Colour and Trim Options, 2011 Models

There were sixteen different paint choices available during the 2011 model-year, although the maximum available at any one time was thirteen. There was one substitution in January 2011. Three of the 2010 colours were not carried over, and Baltic Blue replaced Buckingham Blue, Fuji White replaced Alaska White, and Siberian Silver replaced Izmir Blue.

From May 2011, six colours became unavailable as paint supplies were disrupted after the Japanese earthquake. Two of these were replaced by similar options (Sumatra Black replaced Santorini Black, and Orkney Grey replaced Stornoway Grey).

All these paints were metallic types except for Fuji White, which was a traditional 'solid' type.

As in 2010, there were three styles of upholstery: leather, Premium leather, and leather with Alcantara wearing surfaces. Colour availability was as follows:

Standard leather:	Almond, Ebony, Ocean
Premium leather:	Almond, Arabica, Ebony, Ivory, Tan
Leather with Alcantara:	Almond/Nutmeg, Ebony/Lunar, Ivory/Ocean, Ivory/Lunar

The optional extended leather pack added leather to the four door armrests and top rolls, the dashboard top, the instrument panel peak and the end caps of the dashboard. The dashboard top was finished either in Ebony or to match the seat upholstery.

The three varieties of wood-trim panel were carried over from 2010, and were Anigre (gloss), Grand Black Lacquer (gloss) and Straight Grain Walnut (with a satin finish).

The interior options were again grouped into six 'colourways'. These were as follows:

Almond/Nutmeg:	Almond seats with Nutmeg carpet; or Almond and Nutmeg seats with Nutmeg carpet. Straight Grain Walnut wood was the designer's choice.
Arabica/Almond:	Arabica seats with Nutmeg carpet. Anigre wood was the designer's choice.
Ebony:	Ebony seats with Ebony carpet; or Ebony and Lunar seats with Ebony carpet. Grand Black Lacquer wood was the designer's choice.
Ebony/Ivory:	Ivory seats with Ebony carpet; or Ivory and Lunar seats with Ebony carpet. Grand Black Lacquer wood was the designer's choice.
Ebony/Tan:	Tan seats with Ebony carpet. Grand Black Lacquer wood was the designer's choice.
Ocean/Ivory:	Ocean seats with Ocean carpet; or Ivory seats with Ocean carpet; or Ivory and Ocean seats with Ocean carpet. Anigre wood was the designer's choice.

Most combinations were feasible, although as always Land Rover did not provide some combinations that they considered did not work; in sales catalogues they also highlighted

COLOUR AND TRIM OPTIONS

Paint	Codes	Notes
Bali Blue	823, JBL	Suspended in May 2011. Not available with Almond/Nutmeg or Ebony/Tan colourways. Designer's choice was the Ebony colourway
Baltic Blue	912, JEB	Suspended in May 2011. Designer's choice was Ivory seats with Ebony carpet
Bournville	822, AAD	Not available with the Ocean/Ivory colourway. Designer's choice was the Arabica/Almond colourway
Fuji White	867, NDH	Designer's choice was the Ocean/Ivory colourway
Galway Green	821, HAC	Designer's choice was the Almond/Nutmeg colourway
Ipanema Sand	824, GAQ	Designer's choice was the Ebony/Ivory colourway
Izmir Blue	920, MWE	To January 2011 only. Designer's choice was the Ebony colourway
Marmaris Teal	826, JCK	Designer's choices were Ivory seats with Ocean carpets, or Ivory and Ocean seats with Ocean carpets
Nara Bronze	825, AAJ	Suspended in May 2011. Designer's choice was the Arabica/Almond colourway
Orkney Grey	949, LJZ	Substitution for Stornoway Grey, May 2011. Interior options not advertised, but probably the same
Rimini Red	889, CBK	Suspended in May 2011. Not available with Ocean/Ivory colourway. Designer's choice was the Almond/Nutmeg colourway
Santorini Black	820, PAB	Suspended in May 2011. Designer's choices were the Ebony/Ivory and Ebony/Tan colourways
Siberian Silver	834, MBP	From January 2011. Designer's choice was Ocean seats with Ocean carpets
Stornoway Grey	907, LEL	Suspended in May 2011. Designer's choice was the Ebony colourway
Sumatra Black	797, PBF	Substitution for Santorini Black, May 2011. Interior options not advertised, but probably the same
Zermatt Silver	798, MBK	Designer's choices were Ocean seats with Ocean carpets, and the Ebony/Tan colourway

WHEEL AND TYRE OPTIONS, 2011 MODEL-YEAR

Specification	Style	Description
	Style 1	19in × 9J with five V-spokes, Sparkle Silver finish and 255/50R19 tyres
SE and HSE	Style 3	20in × 9.5J fifteen-spoke with Sparkle Silver finish and 275/40R20 tyres
	Style 4	20in × 9.5J fifteen-spoke with diamond-turned finish and 275/40R20 tyres
	Style 5	19in × 9J fifteen-spoke with 255/50R19 tyres
Supercharged	Style 6	20in × 9.5J five-spoke with 275/40R20 tyres
	Style 7	20in × 9.5J five-spoke with diamond-turned finish and 275/40R20 tyres
Autobiography	Style 8	20in × 9.5J ten-spoke with diamond-turned finish and 275/40R20 tyres

the ones they thought worked best by describing them as 'designer's choice' options.

Wheel and Tyre Options, 2011 Model-Year

Centre caps normally carried a gold-on-green Land Rover logo, but those for the Supercharged models were silver on black.

THE 2012 MODELS: THE SDV6

The focus for the 2012 model-year was on yet another new engine, a further development of the 3.0-litre TDV6 that was known as the SDV6. With 256PS, it offered sparkling performance and just 12PS less than the old TDV8 – which in turn helped to explain why the bigger diesel engine had needed such a major re-work in order to remain a useful element in the range. One aim of the 6-cylinder diesel's development programme had, of course, been to meet the EU5 emissions regulations, and to that end a new low-flow fuel injection system was used.

The SDV6 models were announced in July 2011, and kicked off the 2012 model-year for the Sport. Central to their development programme had been a new eight-speed ZF automatic gearbox (although other models retained the old six-speed type for 2012). This new gearbox was called the 8HP70. It had a taller overdrive top gear than before, and incorporated a number of sophisticated new energy-saving features. There was a transmission idle control, which automatically selected neutral when the car was standing for a time idling in gear. Links to other on-board systems allowed the gearbox to select a lower gear in hot conditions to run the engine and therefore the air-conditioning pump faster in order to cool the cabin down more quickly; similarly, in cold weather the same system ran the engine faster to reduce warm-up time and emissions.

The gearbox adapted its shift patterns to the driver's style, too (Land Rover called this 'Driver Type Detection'); it had a curve detection feature, which would hold a gear through a series of bends to prevent unwanted upchanges, and could also monitor the driver's use of the brake pedal and the rate of deceleration in order to choose the correct gear for entry into a corner and exit from it. Also new was its ability to change from one gear to another without having to run sequentially through all the intervening gears: if necessary, it could change directly from first to eighth, skipping the six ratios in between altogether.

The driver-facing controls for the eight-speed gearbox were also new, with steering-wheel paddle-shift controls (branded as 'Drive Select') and a rotary selector not dissimilar to the one used for the Terrain Response system on Land Rover's latest models. It must be said that not everybody liked this rotary gear selector, which was introduced to reduce clutter on the centre console in the same way that the electronic handbrake had been intended to do.

With the SDV6 models came a new lightweight, aluminium, single-piece powered tailgate, which could be opened from the facia, the key fob, or from the tailgate itself. With this new tailgate, the Range Rover nameplate moved to a new position below the rear window, and a bright strip was added underneath it. Exterior enhancements included silver-on-black Range Rover branding for the wheel centres on all models, and there was the usual seasonal revision of the paint options – but this time it was accompanied by a sly marketing trick. Five of the colours new for 2012 were described as 'Premium' types, which meant that they had to be ordered specially, and cost extra.

The three main types of upholstery were renamed, as Standard leather became Grained leather, Premium leather became Oxford leather, and the leather and Alcantara combination became Partial leather. Oxford leather could be had with a contrast stitch, and a carbon-fibre option was added to the otherwise all-wood selection of trim finishes. Further interior design revisions included the introduction of an HSE luxury pack, a 'Say What You See' voice command system, a dual view touch screen (as on the full-size Range Rover), an 825-watt Premium harmon/kardon LOGIC 7 audio system, and WhiteFire wireless technology for the optional rear-seat entertainment system, which had an 8in screen in the back of each front seat headrest.

The Autobiography equipment level was now available with seven exterior colours – one more than in the 2011 model-year – and these were Baltic Blue, Firenze Red, Fuji White, Indus Silver, Nara Bronze, Orkney Grey and Santorini Black. However, there were several new interior options, and the 2011 selection of Le Mans, Monaco and Monza was joined by four more: Cannes, Estoril, Hockenheim and Valencia.

As for engines, British buyers were once again offered just two choices: the supercharged V8 and the SDV6 diesel. However, the 5.0-litre petrol V8 and the 4.4-litre TDV8 remained in production for overseas markets.

The highlight of the 2012 model-year was the new **SDV6** engine with eight-speed gearbox, although whether that is what was actually fitted to the Sport in this publicity picture is open to question.

The 19in Style 5 alloy wheels with their fifteen-spoke design give this 2012-model Sport an air of distinction.

Dutch Dynamic Edition

The Dutch market was treated to a special-edition Sport in early 2012 that was called the Dynamic. This was an SDV6 model with gloss black finish for the radiator grille and wing vents, and with Style 7 alloy wheels that combined gloss black spokes and diamond-turned highlights. The upholstery was in Ebony perforated leather with Ivory contrast stitching.

ABOVE LEFT: **A Diamond-turned finish was used to good effect on the Style 7 alloy wheels.**

ABOVE RIGHT: **Gloss Black side vents and Style 7 wheels featured on the Dynamic Edition.**

The upholstery of the Dynamic Edition was in Ebony with Ivory contrast stitching.

New Options for 2012

Even though the main focus of Land Rover's product activity for 2012 was on the new Range Rover Evoque, there were still some new options for the L320 Sport. These included Range Rover-branded valve caps, daytime running lights in the lower edge of the front bumper, and a rotary gearshift upgrade, bringing the rotary selector to models other than the SDV6. For the load space, there were also new luggage rails and a luggage retention net.

WHAT THE PRESS THOUGHT

The Sport was now old enough not to command many road tests in the media any more, but *Autocar* magazine did try out one of the new SDV6 models for its issue dated 9 November 2011. The report made clear that L320 had lost none of its appeal: the magazine concluded that 'the Range Rover Sport is a glorious way to cover long distances effortlessly and rapidly, and it works as a luxury car better than nearly any conventional saloon.' The report also said:

[It was] …a compelling way to travel. The imperious driving position, superb forward visibility and very brisk performance are a seductive mix. [The car was] …always stable and confidence-inspiring, allowing the driver to focus on enjoying the ride, the view, or the car's ability to stride past slower-moving vehicles. Indeed, the trademark express-train Range Rover overtaking manoeuvre has to be one of today's definitive driver experiences…. The ride only rarely betrays a slight knobbliness, and the steering… has an accuracy and weighting that are pretty impressive for a vehicle of this type.

As for the new engine, *Autocar* found it 'very refined and seamlessly torquey,' and recorded a 200km/h (124mph) top speed with 8.5sec for the 0–60mph sprint. The eight-speed gearbox was 'swift and unobtrusive' – although on this low-mileage press demonstrator 'it occasionally hung on to too high a gear at very low speeds, and was keen to shift into top at higher speeds.'

The magazine admitted that 'the extraordinary off-road ability is probably surplus to most requirements, but once you've experienced the Sport crawling down a 45-degree slope, you can't help admiring it even more.'

Land Rover never lost sight of the Sport's genuine ability off-road – this was one of a series of pictures taken at the company's Eastnor Castle proving ground to underline the fact.

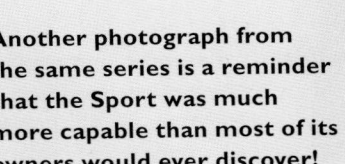

Another photograph from the same series is a reminder that the Sport was much more capable than most of its owners would ever discover!

For 2012, it was possible to have the daytime running lights embedded in the spoiler – an accessory available only through Land Rover dealers.

The devil is in the detail – and it certainly was with these accessory tyre valve covers.

The Future Car Challenge

Land Rover gained a few extra column inches in the press by entering three of the Range_e concept prototypes into the RAC Future Car Challenge, which took place on 5 November – the day before the RAC's famous London-to-Brighton Veteran Car Run. The event drove the traditional 96km (60-mile) Veteran Run route in reverse, starting at Brighton, and the challenge was to complete the distance using the least energy possible within the 2hr 45min minimum and 3hr 30min maximum time permitted.

The Range_e was nevertheless up against some formidable competition, and did not win any prizes in an event where the star entry was the T.27 city car from Gordon Murray Design, which averaged an equivalent of 0.8ltr/100km (350mpg).

A French Special Edition

Land Rover's French national sales company was a past master at creating special editions to boost sales at strategic points in the year, and in November 2011 French buyers were offered an Eden Park edition. This followed on from an Eden Park special edition of the Defender that had been released in July.

Eden Park was a Parisian clothes manufacturer, and each example of the Range Rover Sport Eden Park Edition came with an accessory pack that consisted of a leather sports bag, a rugby ball and a blue polo shirt. It is not clear how many examples of the Eden Park were built (the equivalent Defender continued into 2014, in line with demand), but each one did carry a numbered plaque inside the passenger cabin.

The Eden Park edition could be had in just four colours – Buckingham Blue, Fuji White, Indus Silver and Sumatra Black – and in each case had a gloss black grille and side vents, plus an Eden Park logo on the left side of the tailgate. (The availability of Sumatra Black suggests that these might have been late 2011 models rather than 2012 types, and that the edition had been created as a way of clearing stocks of old models.) With all four colours, the interior was in Ebony perforated leather with contrast stitching in Cirrus, Pimento or Scuba.

One of the Range_e experimental vehicles on the route of the RAC Future Car Challenge.

Two Special Variants of the Sport: HSE Red and HSE Luxury

Land Rover announced two new special variants of the Sport at the New York Show in April 2012, although actual availability in Britain began in June. These were not limited editions, but simply variants designed to offer a higher degree of personalization. They deliberately appealed to two different key areas of the target customer group, and were called the HSE Red and the HSE Luxury. Both had the same showroom price, and came with the SDV6 diesel engine and eight-speed automatic gearbox.

The HSE Red was the brasher of the two models. It was not actually red, but had a Salsa Red badge on the tailgate and a red logo bar on each front wing vent. These vents had Santorini Black meshes with an Atlas Silver surround, and similar colours were carried over to the radiator grille, which had a Santorini Black mesh highlighted by a Noble bezel and black surround. Bonnet badges and tailgate finisher were in Atlas Silver, and there were just four paint colour options: Firenze Red, Fuji White, Orkney Grey and Santorini Black. Wheels were a unique 20in five-spoke design with a Diamond-turned finish.

The interior came with the HSE Ebony colourway, with a choice of four colours for the centre panels: Cirrus, Ebony, Lunar Grey or Pimento Red, in each case with contrast

The special tailgate badge used on the HSE Red edition…

stitching. All headrests had an embossed Sport logo, and this was picked up on the floor mats, which had the logo embroidered in red. Grand Black Lacquer wood trim was standard inside the passenger cabin, and a seventeen-speaker, 825-watt LOGIC 7 sound system was standard.

The HSE Luxury was deliberately more discreet, and was aimed at the customer whose focus was on the comfort afforded by the Sport rather than on its image. This

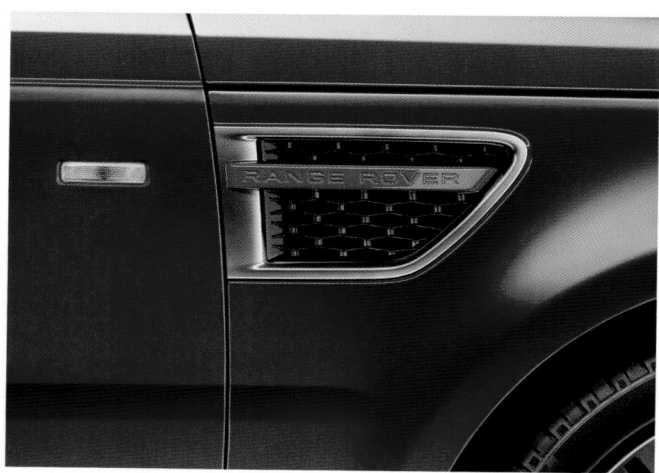

... and the special side vent of the HSE Red.

The Style 14 wheel, available only for the HSE Red models.

There were even special footwell mats for the HSE Red, with the Sport name appropriately picked out in bright red.

The Sport name figured on the headrests of the HSE Luxury model...

also had 20in alloy wheels in a unique style – Style 6, in this case – and the LOGIC 7 sound system. However, it had 'HSE Luxury' badging, and came with the extended leather package, contrasting seat stitching, and a heated steering wheel.

Colour and Trim Options, 2012 Models

There were sixteen different paint choices available during the 2012 model-year, of which five were extra-cost 'Pre-mium' options. All were metallic paints except for Fuji White, which was a traditional solid colour.

Eight of the 2011 colours became unavailable, as Bali Blue, Bournville, Galway Green, Izmir Blue, Rimini Red, Storno-way Grey, Sumatra Black and Zermatt Silver were retired. Three new standard colours were introduced – Aintree Green, Firenze Red and Indus Silver – together with the five Premium options – Barolo Black, Barossa, Causeway Grey,

... and this Ebony with Pimento upholstery was one of the options.

Havana and Mariana Black. Orkney Grey had been available late in the 2011 model-year as a substitute when supplies of Stornoway Grey dried up.

There were now five styles of upholstery: cloth, grained leather, partial leather, partial leather with contrast stitch, Oxford leather, and Oxford leather with contrast stitch. Colour availability was as follows:

Cloth:	Ebony
Grained leather:	Almond, Ebony, Ocean
Partial leather:	Almond/Nutmeg, Ebony/Lunar, Ivory/Ocean, Ivory/Lunar
Oxford leather:	Almond, Arabica, Ebony, Ivory, Tan

The optional extended leather pack added leather to the four door armrests and top rolls, the dashboard top, the instrument panel peak and the end caps of the dashboard. The dashboard top was finished either in Ebony or to match the seat upholstery.

The three varieties of wood-trim panel were carried over from 2011, and were Anigre (gloss), Grand Black Lacquer (gloss) and Straight Grain Walnut (with a satin finish). There was a fourth option, which was Carbon Fibre.

The interior options were grouped into the same six 'colourways' as in the 2011 model-year. These were:

Almond/Nutmeg:	Almond seats with Nutmeg carpet; *or* Almond and Nutmeg seats with Nutmeg carpet. Straight Grain Walnut wood was the designer's choice.
Arabica/Almond:	Arabica seats with Nutmeg carpet. Anigre wood was the designer's choice.
Ebony:	Ebony seats with Ebony carpet; *or* Ebony and Lunar seats with Ebony carpet. Grand Black Lacquer wood was the designer's choice.
Ebony/Ivory:	Ivory seats with Ebony carpet; *or* Ivory and Lunar seats with Ebony carpet. Grand Black Lacquer wood was the designer's choice.
Ebony/Tan:	Tan seats with Ebony carpet. Grand Black Lacquer wood was the designer's choice.

COLOUR AND TRIM OPTIONS

Paint	Codes	Notes
Aintree Green	866, HGY	Designer's choice was the Almond/Nutmeg colourway
Baltic Blue	912, JEB	Designer's choice was Ivory seats with Ebony carpet
Barolo Black	861, PEH	Premium. Not available with the Ocean/Ivory colourway
Barossa	871, KEB	Premium. Not available with the Ocean/Ivory colourway. Designer's choice was the Almond/Nutmeg colourway
Causeway Grey	869, GAA	Premium. Designer's choice was the Ebony/Ivory colourway
Firenze Red	868, CAH	Not available with the Ocean/Ivory colourway. Designer's choice was Ebony seats with Ebony carpet
Fuji White	867, NDH	Designer's choice was Ivory or Ivory/Ocean seats with Ocean carpet
Havana	865, AAN	Premium. Designer's choice was the Arabica/Almond colourway
Indus Silver	863, MEN	Designer's choices were Ocean seats with Ocean carpet, or the Ebony/Tan colourway
Ipanema Sand	824, GAQ	Designer's choice were the Ebony/Ivory and Almond/Nutmeg colourways
Mariana Black	860, PEL	Premium
Marmaris Teal	826, JCK	Designer's choice was Ivory or Ivory/Ocean seats with Ocean carpet
Nara Bronze	825, AAJ	Designer's choice was the Arabica/Almond colourway
Orkney Grey	949, LJZ	Designer's choice was the Ebony colourway
Santorini Black	820, PAB	Designer's choice was the Ebony/Ivory colourway
Siberian Silver	834, MBP	Designer's choice was Ocean or Ocean/Ivory seats with Ocean carpet

Ocean/Ivory: Ocean seats with Ocean carpet; *or* Ivory seats with Ocean carpet; *or* Ivory and Ocean seats with Ocean carpet. Anigre wood was the designer's choice.

Most combinations were feasible, although as always Land Rover did not provide some combinations that they considered did not work; in sales catalogues they also highlighted the ones they thought worked best by describing them as 'designer's choice' options.

The special Autobiography interior colour combinations are shown in the box to the right.

AUTOBIOGRAPHY INTERIOR COLOUR COMBINATIONS

Cannes	Ivory with Ebony
Estoril	Ebony with Cirrus
Hockenheim	Ebony with Lunar
Le Mans	Ebony with Tan
Monaco	Ebony with Ivory
Monza	Ebony with Pimento
Valencia	Arabica with Almond

Wheel and Tyre Options, 2012 Model-Year

All the centre caps had Range Rover branding. There were four new line-fit wheel styles for 2012, numbered from Style 9 to Style 14 (though numbers 11 and 13 were omitted), plus one Accessory-only style. The full list was as follows:

WHEEL AND TYRE OPTIONS, 2012 MODEL-YEAR

Style	Description
Style 1	19in × 9J with five V-spokes, Sparkle Silver finish and 255/50R19 tyres
Style 3	20in × 9.5J fifteen-spoke with Sparkle Silver finish and 275/40R20 tyres
Style 4	20in × 9.5J fifteen-spoke with diamond-turned finish and 275/40R20 tyres
Style 5	19in × 9J fifteen-spoke with 255/50R19 tyres
Style 6	20in × 9.5J five-spoke with 275/40R20 tyres
Style 7	20in × 9.5J five-spoke with diamond-turned finish and 275/40R20 tyres
Style 8	20in × 9.5J ten-spoke with diamond-turned finish and 275/40R20 tyres (Autobiography only)
Style 9	20in nine-spoke with 275/40R20 tyres
Style 10	20in nine-spoke with polished finish and 275/40R20 tyres (Autobiography only)
Style 12	20in five-spoke with 275/40R20 tyres
Style 14	20in five-spoke with Shadow Chrome finish and 275/40R20 tyres (HSE Red only)
Accessory	Gloss Black version of Style 7

THE 2013 MODELS: THE RUN-OUT

L320 production was scheduled to end in March 2013 to make way for the new L494 model, and it was no great surprise that the 2013 models were little changed from their 2012 equivalents. Paint and interior options remained the same, too, although there was some variation in the alloy wheel options, as described in the section below.

In Britain, there were just four models available. The entry-level Sport was now the SDV6 SE (for which metallic paint – every colour except Fuji White – cost extra). Above this came the SDV6 Black Edition, which was essentially a variation on the earlier HSE Red but featuring black highlights. Then at the top of the range were two Autobiography Sport models, each with the Exterior Design Pack as standard. The SDV6 Autobiography Sport and the V8 Supercharged Autobiography Sport both came with a choice of seven colours: Baltic Blue, Firenze Red, Fuji White, Indus Silver, Nara Bronze, Orkney Grey and Santorini Black. Interior options were the same as for 2012.

Sales continued unabated, which was a remarkable testimony to the position that the Sport had achieved in the

For the final sales brochures, the Sport was actually pictured on the cover. This one was issued in 2012.

The Sparkle Silver finish is clear on this Style 6 wheel, which displays the bright red housing of the Brembo brake calliper behind. Keeping wheel and calliper looking this good was a demanding task!

market for fashionable performance SUV models. It was also quite remarkable in view of the November 2012 preview of the replacement L494 model at the Los Angeles Show. But the deadline was March 2013. L494 was formally launched at the New York Auto Show that month as a 2014 model, and full production of the new Range Rover Sport began as production of L320 came to an end.

There was no formal ceremony for the media to attend, as often happens when Land Rover ends production of a long-running model. These ceremonies often help to grab a few extra mentions in the media, but there was so much of interest happening elsewhere in the Land Rover product ranges at the time that the public relations team saw no need for such a ceremony to mark the end of the model that had done so much to change public perceptions of the Land Rover brand.

Wheel and Tyre Options, 2013 Model-Year

All the centre caps had Range Rover branding. There was one new line-fit wheel style for 2013, called Style 11, and the Stormer wheels were re-introduced as an accessory-only style. The full list was as follows:

This two-tone upholstery is in a late Autobiography Sport; the headrests carry 'Autobiography Sport' branding.

This was one of the very last **L320 Sports**, an Autobiography model that was displayed at Land Rover's 65th Anniversary celebrations held at Packington Park in April 2013.

WHEEL AND TYRE OPTIONS, 2013 MODEL-YEAR

Style 1	19in × 9J with five V-spokes, Sparkle Silver finish and 255/50R19 tyres
Style 3	20in × 9.5J fifteen-spoke with Sparkle Silver finish and 275/40R20 tyres
Style 4	20in × 9.5J fifteen-spoke with diamond-turned finish and 275/40R20 tyres
Style 5	19in × 9J fifteen-spoke with 255/50R19 tyres
Style 6	20in × 9.5J five-spoke with 275/40R20 tyres
Style 7	20in × 9.5J five-spoke with diamond-turned finish and 275/40R20 tyres
Style 8	20in × 9.5J 10-spoke with diamond-turned finish and 275/40R20 tyres (Autobiography only)
Style 9	20in nine-spoke with 275/40R20 tyres
Style 10	20in nine-spoke with polished finish and 275/40R20 tyres (Autobiography only)
Style 11	20in five-spoke in Gloss Black with diamond-turned highlights and 275/40R20 tyres
Style 12	20in five-spoke with 275/40R20 tyres
Style 14	20in five-spoke with Shadow Chrome finish and 275/40R20 tyres (HSE Red only)
Accessory	Gloss Black version of Style 7
Accessory	20in × 9.5J Stormer with nine spokes, Titan Silver finish and 275/40R20 tyres

Technical Specifications, 2011–2013

Engines

(1) TDV6 3.0-litre diesel
2993cc (84 × 90mm) Ford-Peugeot ohv V6 diesel with 4 valves
    per cylinder, common-rail injection, twin parallel sequential
    turbochargers and intercooler (EU5 compliant)
Bosch Gen 3 engine-management system
16:1 compression ratio
245bhp at 4,000rpm
442lb/ft at 2,000rpm

(2) SDV6 3.0-litre diesel (2012–2013 models)
2993cc (84 × 90mm) Ford-Peugeot ohv V6 diesel with 4 valves
    per cylinder, common-rail injection, twin parallel sequential
    turbochargers and intercooler (EU5 compliant)
Bosch Gen 3 engine-management system
16:1 compression ratio
255bhp at 4,000rpm
442lb/ft at 2,000rpm

(3) 4.4-litre TDV8 diesel
4367cc (84 × 98.5mm) Ford-Land Rover ohv V8 diesel with
    4 valves per cylinder, common-rail injection, twin parallel
    sequential turbochargers and intercooler (EU5 compliant)
16.1:1 compression ratio
308bhp at 4,000rpm
516lb/ft from 1,500–3,000rpm

(4) 5-litre Jaguar V8 petrol
5000cc (92.5 × 93mm) Jaguar-Land Rover LR-V8 petrol V8
    with four camshafts and 4 valves per cylinder
9.5:1 compression ratio
375bhp at 6,000rpm
375lb/ft at 2,500rpm

(5) 5-litre supercharged V8 petrol
5000cc (92.5 × 93mm) Jaguar-Land Rover LR-V8 petrol V8
    with four camshafts and 4 valves per cylinder plus Eaton
    twin-vortex supercharger and intercooler
9.5:1 compression ratio
510bhp at 6,000rpm
460lb/ft at 2,500rpm

Transmission
Permanent four-wheel drive with centre differential
    incorporating viscous coupling to give automatic locking;
    Terrain Response traction system standard; optional locking
    rear differential

Final drive ratio: 3.73:1 (V8 petrol models)
                         3.54:1 (TDV6, TDV8 and V8 Supercharged
                         models)

Primary gearbox:
Six-speed ZF 6HP28 automatic (TDV6, TDV8, V8 and
    supercharged V8); ratios 4.171:1, 2.340:1, 1.521:1, 1.143:1,
    0.867:1, 0.691:1, reverse 3.403:1

Eight-speed ZF 8HP70 automatic (SDV6 only); ratios 5.000:1, 3.200:1, 2.143:1, 1.720:1, 1.314:1, 1.000:1, 0.822:1, 0.640:1, reverse 3.456:1

Transfer gearbox:
Separate two-speed type with 'active' centre differential; high ratio 1:1, low ratio 2.93:1

Suspension
Independent front and rear suspension with height-adjustable electronic air suspension and telescopic dampers; double wishbones front and rear

Steering
ZF Servotronic speed proportional power-assisted rack and pinion

Brakes
Four-wheel disc brakes with dual hydraulic line, servo assistance and Bosch four-channel ABS
Ventilated front discs with 360mm diameter and twin-piston sliding callipers (TDV6, SDV6 and TDV8), or 380mm diameter with six-piston fixed callipers (supercharged V8)
Ventilated rear discs with 350mm diameter and single-piston sliding callipers (TDV6, SDV6 and TDV8), or 365mm diameter with single-piston sliding callipers (supercharged V8)
Servo-operated parking brake operating on drums within the rear discs

Vehicle dimensions

Wheelbase:	2,745mm (108.1in)
Overall length:	4,788mm (188.5in)
Overall width:	1,928mm (75.9in); 2,170mm (85.4in) over mirrors
Overall height:	1,817mm (71.5in) at standard ride height
Unladen weight (for typical UK-market models):	(1) 3.0-litre TDV6 and SDV6 models: 2,535–2,670kg (5,588–5,886lb) (2) 5.0-litre supercharged V8 models: 2,590–2,679kg (5,710–5,906lb)

Performance
(1) 3.0-litre TDV6 models
Max. speed: 193km/h (120mph)
0–60mph: 8.8sec

(2) 3.0-litre SDV6 models
Max. speed: 200km/h (124mph)
0–60mph: 8.5sec

(3) 5.0-litre petrol V8 models
Max. speed: 210km/h (130mph)
0–60mph: 7.2sec

(4) 5.0-litre V8 Supercharged models
Max. speed: 225km/h (140mph)
0–60mph: 5.9sec

CHAPTER SEVEN

BUILDING THE RANGE ROVER SPORT

Every L320 Range Rover Sport was built at Land Rover's Solihull factory in the Midlands, and no arrangements were ever made for CKD assembly overseas – although overseas assembly was used to supplement domestic build for some other Land Rover products.

As explained in Chapter 2, Land Rover created a completely new assembly building for the Range Rover Sport and the related L319 Discovery 3, and also built a new Body In White (BIW) plant that assembled the bodyshells for both models. This plant had been assembling Discovery 3 models for around a year before the start of Range Rover Sport production, but the second model was integrated seamlessly into the assembly operation, which was an extremely impressive sight. Land Rover were sufficiently proud of it to include visits to the Body In White and T5 Trim and Final areas in some of their visitors' tours of the Solihull plant, run by the Land Rover Experience business unit.

The L320 Sport was, of course, not entirely manufactured at Solihull. As was standard practice for Land Rover, many of its component parts were manufactured off site and brought into the Solihull factory by road, there being no rail link to do the job. In earlier times it had been standard practice to have large component storage areas alongside the assembly lines, but for the two T5 models a computer-controlled 'Just

The Sport was made at Land Rover's traditional home in Solihull.

In Time' system had almost eliminated this expensive waste of factory space, replacing it with 'buffer zones' where small stocks of items were kept – just enough in each case to cater for fluctuations in line speed. Under this system, it was the responsibility of Land Rover's suppliers to deliver the items required on time, and there were penalty clauses in their contracts to discourage defaulters.

CHASSIS AND POWERTRAIN

Among the major components brought into the factory from outside were the chassis frames, which came from the Wolverhampton factory owned jointly by GKN and the American Dana Corporation. As explained in Chapter 2, this factory was specially built to use the hydro-forming process that Dana had developed, where malleable steel is put into a mould and forced into shape by liquid injected at very high pressure. The process delivered very accurate results, and also allowed weight to be saved through thinner metal sections in some areas.

Powertrain elements also came into Solihull from outside. Petrol engines came from the Jaguar section within the Ford plant at Bridgend, and diesel engines were delivered from the Ford plant at Dagenham. There was an international element, too: primary gearboxes were shipped in from ZF at Friedrichshafen in Germany, while transfer boxes came from Magna Steyr in Austria.

All these components were delivered to the T5 Trim and Final building, and at the start of the build process each chassis frame was put on to a moving assembly line that snaked its way up and down the length of the vast assembly hall. Suspension units were bolted on, brake lines were put in, fuel tanks were added, and before long each chassis was ready to receive its major hardware of engine and transmission.

Both Discovery 3 and Range Rover Sport variants of the T5 chassis went down the same lines, sometimes in batches of one type and sometimes as a mixture of types. There were visual differences even at the chassis stage, of course, as the Discovery models had a longer wheelbase than the Sports. However, to ensure that there was never any risk of confusion about what a chassis was to become, or which of the many engine and gearbox options it was to receive, each one had a coded 'build sheet' attached to it. As it passed each assembly station, the associate in charge checked the code for that station and fitted the correct part – which, of course, had been delivered to the lineside with very precise timing, thanks to the computer control systems in place.

Engines for the T5 chassis – both L319 Discovery and L320 Sport – are 'dressed' before being fitted to their chassis.

Automatic gearboxes came in from ZF in Germany. One is seen here receiving fluids before moving off to the chassis assembly line.

THE BODYSHELLS

Meanwhile, bodyshells were taking shape in the Body In White plant. Their construction began with front, middle and rear 'ladder' sections being welded together to make the complete underframe structure of the body. The gaps were then filled in as the floor panels were welded on, making a strong sandwich construction. Next to be added was the front bulkhead – a very important item because all the main dimensions of the Sport's body were taken from it.

The Body In White (BIW) plant had large stillages for the storage of body pressings on their way to be assembled into complete shells. Seen here are body side pressings for the Discovery 3, and bonnets for the L322 Range Rover; the L320 Sport was assembled from pressings in the same way.

In the meantime, the body sides and the rear end were being put together, a process that depended on computer-controlled robot arms that were used to swing huge side panels into position for spot-welding. In each case, the joining of inner and outer panels made another very strong sandwich construction. Roof panels were made by the same principle.

Further down the line, the 'box' of sides, tail panel, headers (bracing the body sides) and roof came together, and its joints were carefully sealed. At this point, the shape of the body became recognizable for the first time. With all the main dimensions fixed, it was now possible to mount the doors, an operation that was again computer controlled to ensure absolute consistency of panel gaps. Front wings were then jig-fitted to the bulkhead, and the bonnet was added, followed by the front panel.

The now complete bodyshell did not stay that way for long. Each shell had its doors removed to improve access to the inside during later stages of the build process. The shells were then whisked away by conveyor up into the roof of the building and out of the BIW plant into the Paint Shop. The doors would also pass through the Paint Shop, and would eventually meet up with their original body again on the Trim and Final line. The perfect fit that the robot assemblers had achieved was guaranteed by leaving the hinge halves in place on the door and body, and removing the hinge pins.

FINAL ASSEMBLY

Rustproofed, primed, and painted with several coats of top colour (plus a lacquer clearcoat to give a final lustre), the newly painted bodies were then brought by overhead conveyor from the Paint Shop into the main assembly hall. Here they began their journey along a first-stage trim line, where dashboards, interior panels and carpets were added, and where glass was fitted by robot arms in a special cell.

Each body was then taken back on to a high-level conveyor in preparation for being mated to its appropriate chassis automatically. In earlier times, the body drop was always one of the most interesting elements of the assembly operation, but for the Sport and its Discovery 3 sibling (and from 2009, Discovery 4), the body was not dropped on to the chassis.

Instead, the chassis was hoisted aloft on its assembly cradle until it met the body on the high-level conveyor. This was a precision operation, in which the two units were very precisely aligned by computer control. The body was then released from its conveyor cradle and the whole assembly was lowered again, moving a stage forwards at ground level to make room for the next pairing. The ten bolts securing body to chassis were done up automatically, and that precise lining up of body and chassis achieved by computer control ensured that bolts and holes lined up first time, every time.

Door-panel pressings for the Range Rover Sport.

On the Trim and Final assembly line, carpeting and other interior items are assembled into the painted bodyshell of a Range Rover Sport.

Overhead slings carry the Range Rover Sport bodyshells along the Trim and Final line. Many of the bodies are silver, grey or black – all popular colours in the middle of the decade when the Sport was launched.

One stage further along the assembly line. This Sport now has its interior trim (though not yet its seats) and most of its wiring harnesses in place. Note that the Range Rover lettering has now been applied to the bonnet. Bonnets normally remained open: this one was probably specially closed for the photographer!

Window glass is added to bodyshells by robots on a glazing cell. Note that the doors are still off the vehicle at this stage.

Sport bodyshells – silver again – are lifted up into the roof of the assembly hall to be moved on to the next stage of the line.

The same operation from a different angle, and one not often seen.

The body and chassis assembly was now picked up in a cradle suspended from another overhead conveyor line, and moved slowly down the final trim line. Seats and other interior trim were installed, and then, thanks again to the computer systems controlling the assembly process, the right set of doors for each vehicle materialized alongside the track and was refitted.

Still suspended by its cradle, each vehicle then moved forwards to be fitted with its wheels, themselves already fitted with tyres. The now complete vehicle was then carried forwards towards a rising ramp where the wheels met the ground for the first time. At the top of this ramp, with the vehicle now standing on its own wheels, the cradle detached itself and returned to the start of the assembly line to pick up another body. The vehicle was then rolled off the ramp to the Engine Control Unit (ECU) calibration area, where the appropriate settings for its destination country and specification were downloaded. Visual quality control checks were also carried out here.

With a battery, water and fuel added, each Sport was started up and driven on to a rolling road, where a number of engine and transmission functions were checked. It then went through a water-spray test, and was driven to a 'sign-off' area where it awaited collection by the Despatch Department, whose job was to send it on its way to the supplying dealership or direct to a customer.

Body has met chassis – which was lifted up to meet it – and the seats have been installed. Clearly visible on the assembly line trolley are the nut runners, which tighten the bolts holding the chassis and bodyshell together. The nearly completed vehicle is now on its way to the final line, where it will be reunited with its doors and fitted with wheels, and then 'bought off' by the Despatch Department.

STATISTICS

The Body In White plant, located at the eastern end of the Solihull site, had a floor area of 48,000sq m (57,400sq yd). At the start of production in 2004 the plant contained 261 robots and employed approximately 630 people, working one day shift and one night shift. Each body took approximately 6.68hr to build, and a new body came off the lines once every 1.64min.

The Trim and Final plant was even larger, with a floor area of 68,000sq m (81,330sq yd). The working space available was greatly increased by the use of the roof space for storage, buffer zones and other conveyor functions. In the early days of production this plant had approximately 1,400 employees, also working a two-shift system. Its annual capacity was 104,000 units, which would, of course, embrace both Range Rover Sport and Discovery models combined, in proportions to suit market demand.

In February 2005, the total assembly time for a Range Rover Sport passing through the Trim and Final line was 6.91hr.

CHAPTER EIGHT

THE NORTH AMERICAN MODELS, 2005–2013

North American customers, and more specifically those in the USA, were fundamental to the original concept of the Range Rover Sport. As explained in Chapter 1, the origins of the model lay in the paired L50 and L51 concepts, which incorporated Land Rover North America's call for a sporty five-seater model. Although the concept evolved far beyond that original idea, the core customer group had been identified some ten years before L320 actually reached the USA.

It was therefore obviously no coincidence that the idea of a sporty Range Rover was first unveiled in the USA, through the appearance of the Range Stormer at the Detroit Motor Show in January 2004. Nor was it a coincidence that the production L320 should have its world première at the Detroit show a year later. And Land Rover's hopes and predictions were not to be disappointed: over the eight-year production life of the first-generation Range Rover Sport, around one in every three examples built would be sold in the USA.

THE 2006 MODELS

Even though the Sport was introduced at a North American motor show, North American sales did not begin before those in other countries. Representatives of the US media were able to sample the new model at the press launch in Catalonia that began in April, and to publish their impressions over the next few weeks. A public relations campaign focused on the USA then began on 24 May in order to build customer anticipation of the new model; the official on-sale date through US showrooms was 30 June 2005.

There was no market at this stage for a diesel-engined model in the USA (although Land Rover certainly had longer-term plans in that area), and so the Sport was sold with a choice between the naturally aspirated and supercharged V8

petrol engines. Side marker lights, integrated within the standard light units, met US traffic regulations, and of course the ICE systems were designed for North American conditions. In other respects, though, the North American Range Rover Sport had no important differences from the versions sold in Europe.

There were three models, called HSE, HSE Lux, and Supercharged, and all models came with a four-year or 80,000km (50,000-mile) warranty. The entry-level HSE model came with satellite navigation as standard, and the HSE Lux added a Cold Climate Pack, adaptive front lighting, and Premium leather and wood (instead of Rhodium plastic) in the cabin. Top of the range was, of course, the Supercharged model, with 20in wheels, Brembo brakes, Dynamic Response suspension and heated sports seats.

The launch was followed up by more intensive promotional work. To gain maximum publicity value from the annual SEMA tuning show held in Las Vegas in November 2005, LRNA decided to put a Sport on display there. However, although a primary theme of this show is performance, and the Sport certainly had plenty of that, it is also very largely about customizing and tuning. In that context, an unmodified Sport would not have been an appropriate exhibit, and so LRNA decided to create one that would be appropriate.

They therefore had a Supercharged model customized by Troy Lee Designs, a company based in Corona, California, and best known for its custom paintwork on such items as motorcycle helmets. This model was given an eye-catching individual paint job that was said to have been inspired by the 'technicolours of Las Vegas', and a host of hand-crafted custom details were added. The result attracted plenty of the desired attention while it was on display at the show, but there was more publicity to be gathered from it later, and on 18 April 2006, the Troy Lee Sport was sold off at a closed

ABOVE LEFT: **The Troy Lee Design Sport made LRNA's new model eligible for the SEMA tuning show in November 2006, and kept up a relentless publicity campaign.**

ABOVE RIGHT: **The vehicle's identity was displayed prominently on the rear of the Troy Lee Sport – far more so than on the standard models. The privacy glass all round added to the effect, and over the next few years many US customers specified privacy glass (though usually for the rear only) on their Sports.**

auction for Range Rover retailers. It was bought by Jerry De Souza, the General Sales Manager of Land Rover Anaheim Hills. He was reported to have paid $96,000 for it – at a time when the standard Supercharged model cost just under $70,000. The difference may not have quite covered LRNA's bill for having the vehicle customized in the first place!

All this played out against a nation-wide TV advertising campaign that had begun on 30 January 2006, and was followed up by a press campaign in February. The campaign was called *Designed for the Extraordinary*, and the TV commercials

memorably featured a Sport being driven through a network of aqueducts below the city of Tokyo, where no road-going vehicle had ever been driven before.

The results of this determined publicity were the sales and the public reaction that Land Rover had wanted. In the

Early US promotional activity included a TV campaign called *Designed for the Extraordinary* that featured a Sport being driven through the aqueducts under Tokyo.

WHAT THE PRESS THOUGHT

Automobile **magazine, March 2006:** 'The Sport's ability to crawl across rocks remains almost peerless, and it performs just as well on the straight and level because of its supercharged 390hp, 4.2-liter V8 (borrowed from fellow PAG member Jaguar).'

New York Times, **spring 2006:** 'The Range Rover Sport distinguishes itself with knockout design. If most SUVs are shaped like bricks, the Sport is at least hand-hewn marble, blunt yet elegant.'

A Supercharged Sport starred in the 'Tokyo tunnels' TV campaign.

six months when the Sport was on sale in the 2005 calendar year, LRNA sold 4,656 examples, and in the nine months to the end of September 2006 they sold a further 12,640. The year 2006 was also the first year that the USA overtook the UK as Land Rover's largest world market (although by 2008–2009 the position had reversed).

The Sport attracted awards, too, among them being named Urban Elite SUV of the Year by the AutomotiveRhythms.com web site. And the customers seemed to love them: LRNA's dealer magazine *Articulated* for May 2006 reported on a cus-

The bull bar looks rather incongruous on a Sport, but may well have been a necessity on the Texas ranch where this early, specially camouflaged model did duty.

tomer of the Fort Worth dealership who had bought two Sports: one was in silver and was used for the family's daily commutes, while the other was specially camouflaged and used only on their large Texas ranch.

THE 2007 MODELS

The 2006 model-year had got the Sport off to an excellent start in the USA, but the 2007 model-year was deliberately one of consolidation. The same three L320 models were available as in 2006, although showroom prices edged up a little, and the number of colour options was slimmed down as LRNA got a better feel for what North American customers wanted on their Sports. There were several new items of equipment, too, including a Personal Telephone Integration System with Bluetooth capability as standard, one-touch operation for the front passenger's window, a clock function in the driver's message centre, and some additional options.

It was probably not surprising that Sport sales also slipped in the USA, as this was a deliberately fashionable vehicle and after a year on sale some of the excitement surrounding it had worn off. Nevertheless, Land Rover were probably rather surprised at the extent by which the total fell: in the USA, sales of the Sport dropped to just 35 per cent of their first-year figure, although the drop in Canada was much smaller, to around 80 per cent of the first-year figure. Fortunately, sales around the world were overall still on the increase, and so this disappointing result was something that had to be tackled locally, rather than at Solihull.

THE 2008 MODELS

In time-honoured fashion, LRNA tackled the sales problem during the 2008 model-year with a limited edition that was designed to generate showroom traffic on which the sales force was then expected to build. An increase in showroom prices was to some extent justified by the addition of electric adjustment for the steering column, and by eight-way adjustment for the front passenger's seat in place of the earlier six-way adjustment. Supercharged models could now be ordered with Lux upholstery instead of the standard perforated leather type with sports seats – and the limited edition showcased this. But the same three-tier model range was offered, there was one fewer interior colour option, and only one new paint option was introduced.

Land Rover was expanding its appeal in the **USA** during the 2000s by creating a series of driving experience centres at upmarket resorts. A Sport is seen here at the **Biltmore Driving School** in Asheville, North Carolina.

Much early **US** publicity emphasized the **Sport's** off-road capabilities – which distinguished it from other performance **SUVs** then on the market. This picture was again taken at the Biltmore venue.

There were high-end adventure trips to help promote the brand as well. This picture was taken during one such trip into the Moab national park in Utah.

There were 250 examples of the Supercharged limited edition, which came with the new bodykit, 20in Stormer wheels and automatic cruise control as standard. On the inside, buyers found special tread strips and carpet mats, what LRNA called a 'luxury interior package' (which meant Lux-type seating and upholstery), and a rear-seat entertainment system. This special edition was more or less equivalent to the Sport HST that was sold in Europe during the

ABOVE LEFT: **The sense of adventure was a regular theme in US publicity. This 2008 model was pictured against a backdrop chosen to inspire potential buyers to explore some of America's wilderness.**

ABOVE RIGHT: **This 2008 HSE model displays the 19in wheels that were new for that year.**

RIGHT: **The standard rear view of a 2008 Supercharged model contrasts markedly with the rear view of the Troy Lee 'special' pictured earlier.**

FAR RIGHT: **Greys and silvers were as fashionable in the USA as they were in Europe, despite the availability of several visually more exciting colours.**

ABOVE LEFT: **Black leather and the latest Brunel trim combine in this 2008 model to give an appropriately sporty ambience.**

ABOVE RIGHT: **The rear-seat entertainment system used a screen in the back of each front headrest. It had been an option since the start of Sport sales in the USA.**

2008 model-year (see Chapter 4), and it was the first model for the US market to feature the bodykit that had appeared elsewhere during the 2006 model-year.

One way or another, 2008 saw an upturn in Sport sales. Unsurprisingly, sales in Canada remained much as they had been during 2007, but in the USA they very nearly doubled, and by the summer of 2008 the Sport had become LRNA's best-selling product. Even so, the year's sales total was around just two-thirds of what it had been in 2007, which seems to illustrate that the Sport was viewed in the USA as a high-fashion item that was already beginning to date. This was in fact what Land Rover had always feared might happen – although the effect was much less pronounced outside the USA, where sales were holding up very well indeed.

THE 2009 MODELS

Unfortunately, the effects of the global recession were felt very keenly in the USA during the 2009 model-year, which turned out to be the worst ever year for the Sport in North America. Sales dropped to around 43 per cent of their 2008 total and, as the detailed table later in the chapter shows, there were six months during which no sales at all of the Range Rover Sport were reported. At other times this would have been catastrophic, but of course the problem was not confined to the Sport, and was not confined to Land Rover: the buyers were simply not there to be found.

Land Rover did what they could to attract customers. Still offering the same three-model range, they widened the choice of paint colours and of interior colour options; they added Noble trim to the vent bezels, the door pulls, and the sides of the centre console; and they added clear tail-light lenses and clear lenses for the side repeaters. They also came up with another special edition and a special equipment package to try to entice customers into the showrooms.

As its name suggests, the HSE Stormer alloy package was aimed at buyers of HSE models. It was almost purely cosmetic, bringing the 20in Stormer alloy wheels that its name suggested, together with a satellite radio tuner (then quite new in the USA) and an interior that boasted premium Ebony leather with Ivory contrast panels, Ebony door inserts with Noble trim, and Noble trim on the console sides. No doubt the package was used as an incentive to avoid heavy discounting in order to gain sales.

The special edition was called the Range Rover Sport HST, and it came with the bodykit, special grille, 20in diamond-turned alloy wheels, automatic cruise control and Lux interior package. It is not clear how many of these were sold, and LRNA were careful not to call it a 'limited' edition because they had every intention of selling as many as they could in very difficult trading conditions.

THE 2010 MODELS

The prospects for the 2010 model-year in the USA looked distinctly brighter. Not only was the economic recession supposedly over, but Solihull had some heavily revised model ranges, and the Range Rover Sport was central to them. In the USA, the L320 model line-up consisted of the same three types as before – HSE, HSE Lux and Supercharged – but there would also be a limited edition to help sales.

Buried deep within documents and memories at Land Rover, there are also clear indications that the company had plans to increase the number of engine options for 2010 until quite late in the game. Diesel engines for the USA had been part of the long-term plan since the development days of L320, as US customers were beginning to warm to the idea of large and powerful diesel engines, thanks largely to the efforts of German car manufacturers. The powerful TDV8 diesel seemed to fit the bill perfectly, and records show that a start was made to building the NAS (North American Specification) Sport TDV8 in July 2009.

However, no such model ever went on sale. The reason may well have been associated with emissions certification for the USA, although Land Rover has made no official comment on the subject. New diesel emissions standards certainly were

due to come into force before long. So one way or another, the TDV8 Sports built in summer 2009 for North America did not go on sale there. It is not clear how many there were, and no doubt all of them were allocated to other left-hand-drive export markets and sold off in the usual way.

There were, of course, multiple new features for the 2010 models that did go on sale in the USA, just as there were for those sold elsewhere (see Chapter 5 for details of these). Interestingly, LRNA highlighted just a small number of specification upgrades in their booklet called *A Retrospective: Land Rover in North America 1985 to 2012*. These were the 'passive entry' and keyless start features and the rear-view camera for the HSE model, and the adaptive front lighting and 'Auto High Beam Assist' specified for the HSE Lux models.

The limited edition for 2010 really was a limited edition, with a defined total of 250 examples. It was called the Range Rover Sport Autobiography, and more or less coincided with the availability of the similarly named special edition in the UK. In much the same way its main purpose was to explore the market for an even more highly equipped model, and to prepare the way for the forthcoming second-generation Sport that was still about three years away from launch.

The North American Autobiography edition had the new 5.0-litre supercharged engine, and came only in Santorini Black. All examples had the 2010 model-year bodykit, 20in Style 8 diamond-turned wheels, the special grille and side-vent mesh, an electronic rear differential lock, automatic cruise control and a special tailgate badge. On the inside, customers got the Extended Leather package in two-tone leather (Ebony with Ivory, Pimento or Tan), with 'Autobiography Sport' embossed on the front-seat headrests and in script on each door insert. An HD digital radio (then considered top-end equipment in the USA) and rear-seat entertainment package were also standard.

THE 2011 MODELS

Sales of the Range Rover Sport for 2010 showed an encouraging improvement over the poor figures for 2009, although they were still not as good as those for 2008, and nowhere near the total achieved in the model's first year on sale in the USA. So for 2011, the US range was refreshed with some changes of colour and repackaged options and features, while showroom prices were held at their 2010 level. There was also another special edition, this one unique to the USA. Sales continued to climb, although

ABOVE LEFT: **A 2011 US model, attractively presented in Rimini Red, shows off the Style 3, fifteen-spoke alloy wheels that really suited the Sport.**

ABOVE RIGHT: **The rear view of the same vehicle makes clear that it is an HSE derivative. The clear lens for the third brake light (in the roof spoiler) on the later models stands out against the red paintwork.**

FAR LEFT: **This publicity picture was presumably intended to show that the Sport could readily be driven off the road on to agricultural land, but it does give the unfortunate impression that the driver has got into difficulties while doing so....**

LEFT: **The suave interior of the later models is well represented by this picture of a 2011 US-model Sport.**

2011 would be the last year in which they would do so in the USA.

For the first time in the North American market there were now four standard trim and equipment levels instead of three. The lower three were the same as before – HSE, HSE Lux, and Supercharged – but the new fourth level was an Autobiography package, following on from 2010's limited edition Autobiography. This consisted of some unique exterior features and an ultra-high level of equipment that included Windsor leather and interior highlights. It became the top equipment level, and was priced at $11,000 above the Supercharged model.

The highlights of the 2011 models included an extended leather package for the HSE Lux and Supercharged models, with contrast stitching on the seats, centre console and door panels. A new Vision Assist package brought adaptive front lighting (that is, swivelling headlights), Automatic High Beam Assist, and the Surround Camera System. The standard audio system was now a 240-watt harmon/kardon type with nine speakers that included a sub-woofer, and the optional premium audio consisted of a 480-watt harmon/kardon system with digital surround sound and thirteen speakers plus a sub-woofer, an HD radio and a satellite radio (the satellite radio being standard on Supercharged models).

The first Range Rover Sport GT edition, which introduced the new bodykit to US customers.

Disappointingly, perhaps, there were no special badges on the GT edition; instead it carried standard 'Sport HSE' identification on the tailgate.

The 2011 special edition was called the Range Rover Sport GT, a name not used in other markets. It came with the naturally aspirated 5.0-litre V8 engine, and was distinguished by what LRNA called a 'special style package' that consisted of the bodykit, 20in Style 6 wheels, and black mesh for the grille and side vents. The upholstery was in Ebony leather with Lunar Alcantara, and there was Anigre gloss wood trim. The climate comfort package was standard, along with a Logic 7 sound system that included SAT and HD radio. No quantities are known for this edition.

LRNA adjusted the paint options at the start of 2011, adding Siberian Silver as an '11.5 model-year' colour, as was done for other countries. The disruption of paint supplies caused by the Japanese earthquake must also have had its effect on US models as well as on those for the rest of the world, although there seems to be no clear acknowledgement of this in LRNA literature.

THE 2012 MODELS

The main news at the start of the 2012 model-year was that NAS Range Rover Sports would now come with gloss black grille and side vents as standard, and black backplates for the head- and tail-lights. As for other markets, a power-operated tailgate and a new compact remote key fob were standard, and the Sport badge moved to the left-hand side of the tailgate.

LRNA's line-up consisted of the same four models as in 2011, all costing a few hundred dollars more than before.

There were also two limited editions to help sales, although it was clear that customer interest in the L320 Sport had now peaked, and the overall sales total for the year was about two-thirds of what it had been for 2011.

The GT limited edition picked up on the success of the 2011 Range Rover Sport GT, and this time was a strictly limited run of 400 examples. Generally similar to the 2011 version, it differed by having Style 7 five-spoke wheels with a diamond-turned finish. The other 2012 limited edition was rather unimaginatively called the HSE Limited Edition, and the quantity was restricted to 350. A key feature was its Style 11 wheels, a 20in size with five spokes and a gloss black finish that had diamond-turned highlights – a design that would not be available elsewhere until the 2013 model-year. The passenger cabin, meanwhile, had an adjustable driver's seat bolster, the climate comfort package, and a LOGIC 7 sound system with SAT and HD radio.

LAST OF THE LINE – THE 2013 MODELS

Paint colours changed for 2013, and the showroom prices of Supercharged and Autobiography models crept up a little further, but there were no major changes. There would have been little point, as the replacement L494 model was only a few months away from becoming available and was previewed at the Los Angeles show in November 2012.

So, with the same four models as for 2012, plus bigger brakes on all models and red callipers for those on

Supercharged types, the L320 Sport entered its final year of availability in the USA. To help the last models through the showrooms before the new Sport went on sale, LRNA fielded two limited editions, the Supercharged Limited Edition and the GT Limited Edition, both available in either black or white.

The Supercharged Limited Edition was the less numerous, and consisted of 500 examples. Of these, 200 were in Fuji White and 300 in Santorini Black, in each case with red highlights similar to those seen on the British HSE Red Edition in 2012 but with carbon veneer Sport badges. There were red highlights inside the cabin, too, plus carbon veneer trim, 'Sport'-branded floormats, and the 825-watt LOGIC 7 sound system.

There were 750 examples of the GT Limited Edition, 300 in Fuji White and 450 in Santorini Black. Both had 20in gloss black wheels, an extended roof spoiler and special chrome exhaust tips. The interior featured a premium audio system and paddle-shifts for the automatic gearbox, but otherwise the GT was based on the HSE model.

RANGE ROVER SPORT SALES IN THE USA

Range Rover Sport sales began in the USA at the very end of June 2005 and the first full month was therefore July 2005. Records suggest that there were no sales at all in August 2008, or between October 2008 and the end of February 2009, as a result of the economic downturn of the time.

The annual sales figures by model-year for L320 in the USA were as follows:

2006	28,575
2007	10,056
2008	19,126
2009	8,176
2010	11,066
2011	16,809
2012	11,470
2013	No figure available

The calendar-year sales figures have been quoted as shown below, but it is hard to reconcile these figures with the model-year figures above. These figures nevertheless give a clearer idea of the impact that the recession had on sales

of L320. The figure for 2013 necessarily includes sales of the first L494 model Sports, and there is no more detailed breakdown available that would show the L320 figures on their own.

2005	10,441 (contrast with the 4,656 quoted in the main text)
2006	18,757
2007	16,989
2008	8,340
2009	9,269
2010	12,347
2011	15,375
2012	17,582
2013	15,976 (see cautionary note, above)

RANGE ROVER SPORT PRICES IN THE USA

The following figures are showroom prices for Range Rover Sport models without extras. All figures are quoted as MSRP

THE RANGE ROVER SPORT IN CANADA

The L320 Sport was, of course, sold in Canada as well as in the USA, and the vehicles had broadly the same specification. Daytime running lights and km/h speedometers were standard on Canadian vehicles, and the warranty ran for four years, or 80,000km (50,000 miles).

Sales were much lower than those in the USA, but were also rather more consistent from year to year. The figures were as follows:

2006	1,161
2007	834
2008	826
2009	651
2010	1,042
2011	1,696
2012	1,103
2013	Total not available

COLOUR AND TRIM OPTIONS 2006–2009

Paint options	2006	2007	2008	2009
Alaska White				x
Arctic Frost	x	x	x	
Atacama Sand				x
Bonatti Grey	x			
Bournville				x
Buckingham Blue	x	x	x	x
Cairns Blue	x			x
Chawton White	x	x	x	
Galway Green				x
Giverny Green	x	x		
Izmir Blue				x
Java Black	x	x	x	
Lucerne Green			x	x
Lugano Teal				x
Maya Gold	x			
Rimini Red	x	x	x	x
Santorini Black				x
Stornoway Grey		x	x	x
Tonga Green	x			
Zambezi Silver	x	x	x	
Zermatt Silver				x
	(Total 11)	(Total 8)	(Total 8)	(Total 13)
Interior options	Alpaca, Aspen, Ebony, Ivory	Alpaca, Aspen, Ebony, Ivory	Alpaca, Ebony, Ivory	Almond, Ebony, Ivory, Nutmeg, Tan
	(Total 4)	(Total 4)	(Total 3)	(Total 5)

RANGE ROVER SPORT PRICES IN THE USA

Model-year	HSE	Supercharged	Autobiography
2006	$56,750	$69,750	
2007	$57,950	$71,250	
2008	$58,500	$71,950	
2009	$59,150	$72,600	
2010	$60,495	$75,395	
2011	$60,495	$75,395	$86,395
2012	$60,895	$76,095	$86,795
2013	$60,895	$76,495	$87,195

('manufacturer's suggested retail price'), and should be regarded as representative and not as definitive for any given vehicle; obviously some customers were able to negotiate discounts.

COLOUR AND TRIM OPTIONS 2006–2013

The tables above and opposite show the options for the NAS Range Rover Sport 2006–2013 in abbreviated form. For further information about combinations of exterior and interior colours, or about paint codes, see the tables in chapters 3, 4, 5 and 6.

COLOUR AND TRIM OPTIONS 2010–2013

Paint options	2010	2011	2012	2013
Aintree Green				x
Alaska White	x			
Bali Blue	x	x	x	
Baltic Blue		x	x	x
Bournville	x	x	x	
Buckingham Blue	x			
Firenze Red				x
Fuji White		x	x	x
Galway Green	x	x	x	
Indus Silver			x	x
Ipanema Sand	x	x	x	x
Izmir Blue	x	x	x	
Lugano Teal	x			
Marmaris Teal		x	x	x
Nara Bronze	x	x	x	x
Orkney Grey			x	x
Rimini Red	x	x	x	
Santorini Black	x	x	(**)	x
Siberian Silver		x	x	x
Stornoway Grey	x	x		
Sumatra Black			(**)	
Zermatt Silver	x	x		
	(Total 13)	(Total 14*)	(Total 14**)	(Total 11)
Interior options	Almond, Arabica, Ebony, Ivory, Nutmeg, Ocean, Tan (Total 7)	Almond, Arabica, Ebony, Ivory, Nutmeg, Ocean, Tan (Total 7)	Almond, Arabica, Ebony, Ivory, Nutmeg, Ocean, Tan (Total 7)	Almond, Arabica, Ebony, Ivory, Lunar, Nutmeg, Ocean, Tan (Total 8)

(*) There were thirteen paint colours available during the last months of 2010; the fourteenth (Siberian Silver) was added at the start of the 2011 calendar year.

(**) Sumatra Black was available only during the period after the Japanese earthquake in 2011 when paint supplies were disrupted. At other times during the 2012 model-year Santorini Black was the black option.

CHAPTER NINE

THE L320 AFTERMARKET SPECIALISTS

From the outset, the Sport was aimed at a new group of customers who in many cases would never have considered a Land Rover product before. The marketing approach was also new, emphasizing style and individuality – 'power and bling' – and the model was quickly picked up by celebrities and others who wanted to drive something that stood out from the crowd. At the wealthier end of this customer group, it was inevitable that customers would try to find ways of making their vehicles that much more individualized, and a big aftermarket soon sprang up to cater for them.

Many of the specialists who served this aftermarket had existed before the Sport arrived on the scene. There had been a tradition of customizing full-size Range Rovers since the 1970s, when it had been kick-started by wealthy buyers in the Middle East, where it was not only expected but also traditional for individuals to make a show of their wealth. Flamboyantly customized cars became another way of doing so, and Range Rovers became particularly popular because they were not only prestigious Western products but also because they were capable of taking their owners into the desert as well as around the cities.

Western buyers of the Sport did not always want this kind of flamboyant customization – although there were many who did. At the entry-level end of the market they typically wanted better road performance, and there were several specialists who could provide that through chip-tuning. Those with a diesel Sport and a little more money to spend visited specialists who extracted more performance by fitting larger intercoolers as well. As an indication of what was available, from December 2008 JE Engineering offered their Stage I tune for the TDV8 engine, which gave the Sport a 0–60mph acceleration time of 7.1sec.

For those who did want flamboyance and a distinctive appearance, the favourite option was larger and more showy wheels, even if these did ruin the ride quality by reducing the depth of the 'cushion' of air that the tyre provided. Land Rover itself recognized this trend, and over the years introduced ever more different and ever larger wheel styles as options. Such wheels were far more vulnerable to kerbing damage than the smaller-diameter types, and would also have been extremely vulnerable in off-road use – but off-road driving was a long way from the aims of the customers who bought them.

Beyond that came bodykits to give a different exterior appearance. It must be said that not all of those made available improved the look of the Sport, but then that was not really the point: their purpose was to make it look different from other Sports, and to get the vehicle and its owner noticed. Some were high-quality fabrications, and others were very much less so, but they all found a market of sorts.

Interior changes tended to be the next stage up in cost, and the main focus was on retrimmed seats and on adding extra gadgets such as high-quality sound systems and entertainment systems with video screens. Land Rover soon caught up with this trend, making special interior colour and upholstery options available, and of course a rear-seat entertainment system was available as a line-built option from the start of production.

Most buyers were content with some combination of these features, and those who wanted a truly individualized vehicle spent as much as their budgets would permit. But right at the top of the aftermarket conversions tree was a very small number of vehicles that were not only customized but also extensively modified. These ranged from stretch limousine conversions to a six-wheeler built for the Middle East, and a two-door coupé that was intended for low-volume production. They were in a different league from the typical showy street conversions that accounted for most of the L320 Sport aftermarket.

Almost every individualized Range Rover Sport was unique, and that was the point. So it would not be possible to list every option that became available. However, the rest of this chapter looks in some detail at the variety that was available, and focuses on the aftermarket specialists who were responsible for these conversions.

FANTOM STYLING

Fantom Styling worked only on Range Rover and Range Rover Sport models, operating out of premises at Long Eaton, Nottingham. The company specialized in cosmetic alterations, including bodykits and wheels, full colour changes,

A pink Range Rover Sport? This one by Fantom was fairly typical, and the registration number was entirely appropriate, too.

Perhaps not looking its best when photographed in a supermarket car park, the Fantom Sport nevertheless represents the company's earlier products.

colour highlighting, and interior retrims using Bridge of Weir leather (as used by Aston Martin and Jaguar, among others). The company continued to work with the L320 Sport long after it had gone out of production, and at the time of writing had recently produced a 'Gen-2' body styling kit.

FARNELL

Yorkshire Land Rover dealers Farnell's were rightly proud of the good-looking special Sport that they completed in summer 2008, and suggested that it might be described as an Autobiography model. Unfortunately, JLR were less impressed, probably because they were already planning to introduce a Range Rover Sport Autobiography special edition in the first quarter of 2010. So Farnell's initiative was not followed up.

GLOHH

Glohh was a specialist automotive light manufacturer, founded in 2011 and focusing on aftermarket business. The company announced its first product for the L320 Sport in February 2014, clearly targeting the owners of Sports who were buying second-hand (the model had gone out of production in March 2013) and who wanted to add some distinctive touches of their own to their new vehicles.

This product was an LED tail-light called the GL-3, which offered a distinctive 'signature' and was a direct swap for the standard tail-light units on both pre- and post-2010 models. In September 2016, the GL-3 was updated as the GL-3 Dynamic, now incorporating a twenty-four LED strip which allowed the light to 'flow' along the indicator segment. A further option in early 2019 was the GL-3X, or X Edition, which came with a darkened lens.

Put together by a Land Rover dealership, the Farnell vehicle showed the possibilities of using standard Land Rover options and accessories, together with a special paint job.

The Glohh tail-lights were very different from the standard production items.

Glohh's GL-3 design incorporated a 'flowing' turn indicator, similar in concept to that seen on some Audi models.

JE ENGINEERING

JE Engineering was a Coventry company that specialized in Land Rover enhancements, and was originally associated with JE Motors, the Rover V8 engine specialists. By autumn 2006, the company had developed a more powerful version of the supercharged V8 engine in the Range Rover Sport, which delivered 434bhp and 622Nm of torque. There were no suspension changes at this stage, but the company's demonstrator sported a set of specially styled alloy wheels.

Auto Express magazine tried an example in November 2006, and reported that it was 'dramatic to drive and amazing to listen to'. The 0–60mph standing-start time was 6.0sec. The estimated cost of such a vehicle was £62,559.

LIMOUSINES

The 'stretch limousine' was a peculiarly American speciality, although many were imported into Europe for specialist private hire work. Typically, these vehicles were converted from standard types by being cut in half and having a long extension inserted. This would then be trimmed and equipped to provide a party room that was usable while the vehicle was travelling.

No, it's not an illusion: this American-built stretch limousine was used by a company in the north of England.
DAVE BARKER/*LAND ROVER ENTHUSIAST*

This limousine was converted by Pinnacle in the USA, whose badge is on the left of the tailgate. The base model was a 4.4-litre US-specification HSE.
DAVE BARKER/*LAND ROVER ENTHUSIAST*

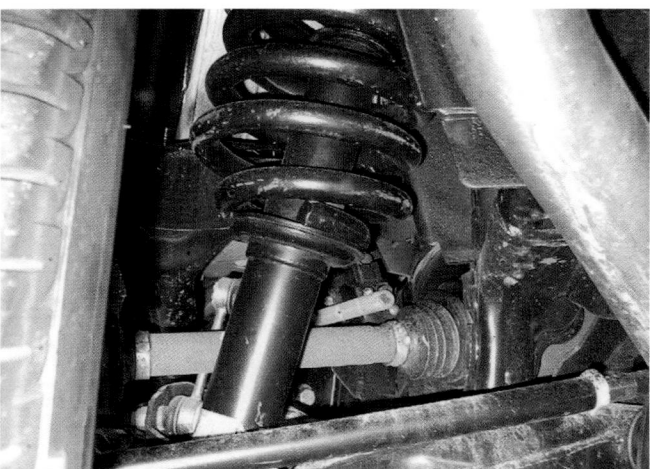

The additional weight also called for some changes. This picture shows one of the coil springs used to reinforce the suspension.
ROGER CONWAY

LEFT: **The additional length of the Pinnacle conversion was supported by a latticework chassis extension, in this picture looking towards the front of the vehicle.**
DAVE BARKER/*LAND ROVER ENTHUSIAST*

The interior could be equipped to suit the client's requirements. This is the interior of the Pinnacle stretch limousine....
DAVE BARKER/*LAND ROVER ENTHUSIAST*

... and this is the interior of a second stretch limousine based on the Sport.
ROGER CONWAY

Among the US specialists was Pinnacle Limousines Manufacturing Inc., a company founded in 1999 that was based at the City of Industry in California. Pinnacle worked with SUVs of all kinds, and had developed a stretch conversion for the Range Rover Sport by mid-2006. The size of the extension could be varied to suit the customer's wishes, but essentially the host vehicle was cut into two between the front and rear doors, and a doorless extension was inserted in the gap. Strength was restored by a latticework of steel members underneath, and the various transmission, brake and electrical services were extended to suit. Steel coil springs replaced the original air suspension to cope with the additional weight. The interior was then trimmed to suit the customer's wishes.

All these vehicles had left-hand drive because of their American origins. Some were exported to Europe, and a few reached Britain as well.

LODER 1899

The German specialist Loder 1899 was (and remains) what the Germans call a 'tuner' – an aftermarket provider of cosmetic and performance conversions for standard vehicles. Based at Odelzhausen in Upper Bavaria, the company specializes in work on Aston Martin, Ford, Jaguar and Land Rover vehicles.

ABOVE: **Modifications to the bumper aprons and changes of wheels were relatively easy to achieve, and made a big difference to the look of the Sport. This one was by Loder 1899, and has the rear privacy glass that became increasingly popular as an option.**

The rear apron on the Loder vehicle has been modified to incorporate large styled exhaust tips.

The Loder enhancements for the Range Rover Sport were announced in April 2006 with the name of Range Rover Sport Black Edition. The central feature was a striking bodykit of front and rear aprons and side sills, the front apron being distinguished by large corner air inlets that incorporated illuminated diodes. At the rear, the corners of the apron had an additional sweep, and there were shaped exhaust outlets.

Loder also offered custom paint highlights in Hyper Silver, and a range of wheels in sizes from 18 to 23in. For customers who wanted extra performance to match the new looks, they could also provide a power increase for the 2.7-litre TDV6 to 220PS from the standard 190PS.

LSE DESIGN

Unique among customized examples of the Range Rover Sport was the Sport Coupé built by LSE Design. That company had been established specifically for the purpose of developing and selling enhancements of Land Rover products, and the Sport Coupé was its first product, announced in February 2008.

The LSE Design Sport Coupé was a two-door conversion of the Range Rover Sport, deliberately recalling the Range Stormer concept of 2004, but with conventional doors instead of the show car's expensive and impractical scissors-type doors. Its makers promised an exclusive run of just 150 cars in 2008, of which the twenty for the UK would be sold only through Stratstone's of Mayfair in London. The prototype was based on a Supercharged Sport and was very extensively modified in the hope of generating customer interest, but the timing of its announcement was very unfortunate. The economic recession that hit the western world in spring 2008 and continued into 2009 undoubtedly damaged its chances of finding buyers, and in the end the project was abandoned – although not until LSE Design had expended a lot of effort on it.

The one and only example built featured extended wings and doors made of steel, and custom metallic paintwork. Both front and rear bumper aprons were specially made, and both incorporated LED lights; the rear apron also carried integral finishers for the stainless-steel 'sports' exhaust system. The roof was re-worked to incorporate a panoramic glass section, and special side runners were added. The Sport's standard suspension was lowered by 30mm (1in) and a set of 22in wheels was fitted, with appropriate low-profile tyres.

On the inside, the seating was changed to resemble that used in the latest Bentley models, with just two 'sports' seats

The LSE Design Sport Coupé is seen here during its conversion, which was done by Custom Exotics of Harlow in Essex. The major exterior conversion, to two-door configuration, has already been done.

The finished article recalled the daring approach taken by the Range Stormer concept. Note the Sport Coupé name on the bonnet, and the huge alloy wheels under flared arches.

BELOW LEFT: **A stylish custom interior made the Sport Coupé a four-seater.**

When the car was re-presented as the Tiret Coupé in 2009, its dashboard looked like this.

in the rear instead of the three-abreast seating in the standard Sport. The seats were all trimmed in Charcoal leather with red suede inserts, and the Coupé name was embroidered on each headrest. There was matching leather for the new door cards, the centre console and the dashboard, plus red inserts on the dashboard to match the upholstery. The headlining was trimmed in Alcantara, and there was a matching blind for the panoramic roof.

The LSE Design Coupé was given the British registration number COU 9E, and later in 2008 was shipped to the

USA for some serious marketing to begin. The strategy was worked out between LSE Design's Andrew Noble and Eric Noble of The Car Lab consultancy in Orange, California, where it was reasonable to suppose that a good number of Coupés would find buyers. It included an intensive programme of events designed to draw attention to the car. Notable among these was the annual Gumball 3000 road rally in August 2008, which invariably attracts a number of celebrities, typically driving supercars. The Coupé was driven by Tyson Beckford (an American actor, model and TV presenter) with actor-comedian Orlando Jones.

Keeping the Coupé in the public eye and riding out the recession must have been high on the agenda during 2009, and LSE Design teamed up with renowned New York jeweller Tiret to give the prototype a diamond-studded instrument panel. Now known as the LSE Design Tiret Coupé, it was displayed at the Baselworld watch and jewellery exhibition in March 2009. Its next major appearance was at the SEMA Show (the initials stand for Specialty Equipment Market Association) in Las Vegas during November, the annual showcase for the modified vehicle industry in the USA.

Things then went quiet for a while, until LSE Design judged that the time was right to re-launch the Coupé during 2012. The prototype was repainted in Grigio Telesto, a light grey from the Lamborghini colour palette, to give it a fresh appearance, and a new round of promotional photo and video shoots began; one video was uploaded to YouTube to gain maximum exposure, and for a time the car had its own web site as well.

Sadly it was all to no avail. LSE Design's timing had been unfortunate once again, and the announcement of the second-generation Range Rover Sport in late 2012 destroyed any hopes of gaining customers for the Coupé. The car was sold into private ownership, losing its distinctive COU 9E registration plate, and in 2018 it was once again for sale by auction.

MANSORY

Mansory Design & Holding GmbH specializes in creating bespoke cars based on prestige luxury and sporting models from a variety of European manufacturers. A key expertise is the design and construction of carbon-fibre parts, but the company also focuses on bespoke interiors and lightweight alloy wheel designs. Its core business is the development and

sale of tuning and accessories for makes that include BMW, Porsche and Range Rover, but it is also well known for its extreme and attention-grabbing motor-show creations, most of which have been hugely expensive one-offs.

The company was founded in Munich in Germany in 1989 by Persian-born Kourosh Mansory, but subsequently moved to Brand, near Bayreuth; it also has a subsidiary at Dübendorf in Switzerland. It has a global dealer network, the British branch being based at Knightsbridge in London since 2017.

The Mansory programme for the L320 Sport was introduced in 2010, and included major makeovers for both exterior and interior, together with an increase in engine power

Carbon-fibre specialists Mansory created a special bonnet for the Range Rover Sport, complete with a large 'power bulge' that acted as an air intake.

Carbon-fibre features were in evidence at the rear of the Mansory vehicle, too.

A superb custom-finished interior added enormously to the appeal of Mansory's work.

for both petrol and diesel models. The exterior featured aerodynamic components made from PU-RIM plastic, and a notable element was the new front spoiler with its vertically arranged LED daytime driving lights and huge air intakes. The engine tuning was matched by a new bonnet with a large power dome that ducted more air into the engine bay, and the rear apron diffuser featured a carbon-fibre insert. A carbon-fibre roof spoiler added to the sporty look, and an option was to have carbon covers for the D-pillars.

OVERFINCH

Overfinch were established players in the Range Rover aftermarket, having started life under the name of Schuler Presses in the mid-1970s. Their focus at that stage was on high-performance conversions of the first-generation Range Rover, with transmission and braking enhancements to match. The company's best-known conversion, and the one on which its reputation was largely based, replaced the original 3.5-litre or 3.9-litre Rover V8 engine by a 5.7-litre Chevrolet V8.

Sold into new ownership in the early 1990s, what was by now Overfinch began to focus increasingly on cosmetic and luxury enhancements in addition to its established performance upgrades. So by the time the Range Rover Sport became available, it was a foregone conclusion that there would be an Overfinch version sooner or later.

Overfinch actually started work in 2005, initially releasing some sketches of Sports wearing bodykits as a 'taster', and in September that year promising a 5.0-litre version of the standard 4.2-litre supercharged V8 in what was called the SuperSport model. This was both bored and stroked, and delivered 500PS at 5,750rpm with 525lb/ft of torque at 3,200rpm; it was also available for the full-size L322 Range Rover. There were to be 22in twelve-spoke Tiger alloy wheels on 9in rims, and an Aerostyling bodykit.

The Overfinch conversion, pictured in 2008. The wheels and bodykit stand out as major changes, but there were almost certainly some performance enhancements for this one as well.

Overfinch offered a performance tune for the TDV8 engine, and with it came special rear badging. The Overfinch name also replaced 'Range Rover' on the tailgate.

The Overfinch exhaust tips and black Overfinch logo are visible here.

Later Overfinch developments produced the **GTS-X**, in this case presented in an eye-catching orange reminiscent of the Range Stormer.

The special side sills and wrap-under rear apron are clear in this picture of the 2012 **GTS-X** model.

The SuperSport became available in March 2006 at a cost of around £40,000 on top of the basic vehicle; the exact figure depended on the degree of custom finishing that the customer requested. A less powerful engine conversion could be achieved with a power pack that added 50PS to the standard 390PS tune by means of a remapped ECU and a tuned supercharger. Bespoke Brembo brakes were also added. The interior was normally retrimmed in a high quality blend of leather and Alcantara.

'Yet more impressive is the noise,' said *Autocar* in its issue of 21 August 2006, after trying the 440PS model. 'I could swear there is a Bristol bomber bellowing behind me. It's the result of freer-flowing quad sports exhausts, and makes the engine produce a brain-crumblingly glorious sound.'

In January 2007, Overfinch announced a performance enhancement for the TDV8 diesel engine used in both the Sport and the full-size Range Rover. This had 321PS and 582lb/ft of torque, and was marketed as the TDV8 GT. Then in the autumn of 2008, the SuperSport package won an award known as the 'Special Recognition for Outstanding Achievement in Design' at the SEMA Show in Los Angeles.

However, the company subsequently ran into financial trouble, and was bought out of administration in 2010 by its Yorkshire distributors, Autobrokers of Leeds. Still trading as Overfinch (Autobrokers had been using the name of Overfinch Leeds), it developed a performance conversion for the later Sport with the 5.0-litre supercharged engine, and introduced this at the Salon Privé event held at London's Syon Park in September 2012. The new Range Rover Sport was, of course, on the horizon by then, but the strategy appears to have been to persuade customers to spend money on upgrading an existing Sport in preference to going for the all-new model.

The Overfinch GTS-X was modified to deliver 575PS (the standard engine delivered 510PS) with 700Nm of torque (as compared to the standard 625Nm). Top speed was claimed as 233km/h (145mph). The GTS-X also had a driver-controlled valve in the exhaust system, which could deliver a spectacular sound where conditions (and the law) allowed. Exterior styling added sculpted side panels, side vents with a gloss black mouthpiece, and two-tone Overfinch lettering on the bonnet and tailgate. Inside there was full Nappa leather upholstery with matching headlining, pillar trims, door cards and boot, plus carbon-fibre leather reveals and copper-orange contrast stitching.

PROJECT KAHN

Project Kahn was (and remains) a brand name of Kahn Design, an automotive fashion company with premises in Bradford, Leeds and London. The company had already focused on enhancements for high-end vehicles such as Aston Martin, Porsche, Mercedes-Benz and Range Rover, and so its involvement with the Range Rover Sport was not unexpected.

The eye-caching colour scheme of the Project Kahn Pace Car inspired a number of copies.

The Project Kahn conversions normally added special badges, seen here on the nose of the bonnet and replacing the standard Land Rover oval on the grille.

A redesigned roof spoiler and special rear apron were also part of the Cosworth model from Project Kahn.

Stage 2 power conversion and 22in RSX forged wheels, which were claimed to be the lightest 22in wheels in the world.

Kahn conversions of the Range Rover Sport were also made available in the USA.

REVERE

The Revere brand was established in London in around 2011, and quickly focused on developing head-turning features for the Range Rover Sport. Among these, the most easily recognizable was a special grille with a large Revere shield badge.

The Cosworth model from Project Kahn added both high performance and a special bodykit and wheels. This publicity picture dates from 2009.

Kahn were quick off the mark with a Stage 1 body-styling prototype for the L320 Sport in 2005, following it up before the end of the year with a Stage 2 version that incorporated the company's new 22in RS-D wheels. Over the next few years, a wide range of options became available, including performance and engineering enhancements, exhaust and suspension systems, plus interior modifications and multimedia systems. A particularly notable model was the Pace Car that was announced in June 2006. Finished in orange with a broad black stripe, this had the company's

Big wheels, a redesigned front apron, and of course special badges identified this Revere conversion.

This was a different front end from Revere, still with their shield badge on the grille and also with the elegant double-R logo behind the headlight lenses.

This view of a Revere HSR model shows the company's treatment of the rear end of the Sport.

That double-R logo appeared again on the side vents.

Revere also offered bodykits, and the repainting of such items as door handles and side vents in the main body colour. The company developed a lowering module for the air suspension to go with its own style of 22in alloy wheels. On the inside there were options for custom gauges and the steering wheel, and for audio-visual equipment, and there was even a set of special umbrellas to go with a Revere Range Rover Sport. Performance enhancements were also on the agenda – as an example, the company offered a 410PS tune for the Supercharged 4.2-litre V8, which had 390PS as standard.

TOTALLY DYNAMIC

The Totally Dynamic approach was very different from that of other companies, as this London company specialized (and still does) in vinyl wraps. For less than the cost of a repaint, a Range Rover Sport could be completely wrapped in vinyl to change its colour. The thinking was that the customer could then afford other colour changes more frequently to suit changes of fashion. The tough vinyl wrap also helped to protect the underlying bodywork against stone chips and similar minor damage, and would leave the paintwork looking unblemished if it was eventually removed.

VANTAGEFIELD

Vantagefield had been providing custom-built Range Rovers and other high-end vehicles for mainly Middle Eastern clients since the mid-1980s, and the company was firmly established as a creator of exotic and expensive bespoke vehicles. By the time of the Range Rover Sport, the demand for customized Range Rovers had diminished – not least because Land Rover was now producing vehicles with much higher levels of equipment straight from the factory – and so the Sport did not figure very often in the Vantagefield repertoire.

A vinyl wrap was the cost-effective solution to a colour change, as demonstrated by this Sport from Totally Dynamic.

In the great tradition of bespoke conversions for the Middle East, Vantagefield produced this extraordinary six-door, six-wheel Sport with twin glass sunroofs.

This Vantagefield conversion was probably the most extreme ever done on an L320 Sport, and remained unique.

The third set of doors of course gave access to a third row of seats.

The load compartment of the six-wheel Vantagefield conversion was also specially laid out.

Nevertheless, in 2009 Vantagefield did produce what might have been the most spectacular Sport conversion ever for a Middle Eastern client. This was a six-door model with three rows of seats, and six-wheel drive as well. It was finished in all-over gold, with twin glass sunroofs, and the interior was entirely upholstered in cloth, which is, of course, more comfortable than leather in a hot climate. The interior was also fitted out with picnic tables and with coolboxes in the extended load space, and there was a built-in gun rack for use when the owner and his friends went hunting in the desert.

VEMIRI

Vemiri Ltd was a Bradford company, established in 2003, and one of the first to provide aftermarket enhancements for the Range Rover Sport. By August 2006 the company was offering a special bodykit, 22in Arnage alloys on 285/35ZR22 tyres, smoked tail-lamps and side repeaters, chromed side vents and front grille, and a quad-pipe stainless-steel exhaust system to dress up the Sport. Also available was an adjustable suspension system, allowing the car to sit 40mm (1.5in) lower than standard at the front and 30mm (1in) lower at the rear.

These options were complemented by interior upgrades that included a Gran Piano Black wood kit for the facia,

A unique bodykit and special wheels made this Vemiri Sport visually distinctive.

A special badge was important to many customers, and Vemiri catered for that.

ABOVE LEFT: **The unique Vemiri tailpipes were branded as well.**

ABOVE RIGHT: **For good measure, Vemiri also offered branded sill plates and carpet overmats.**

branded stainless-steel tread plates and floor- and boot-mats, plus a twin-screen rear entertainment system. Privacy glass in the rear was considered a standard fitting. A further option was a power upgrade for the TDV6 engine from 190PS to 225PS.

The Vemiri upgrades for the Sport seem to have been particularly popular in the area around Bradford. However, Vemiri Ltd ceased to exist after 2010.

WOLFRACE WHEELS

Wolfrace Wheels had long been established as a supplier of aftermarket wheels, and was based in Maldon, Essex. In September 2008, its Wolf Design subsidiary announced a new bodykit for the Sport, featuring new front and rear aprons, fat wheel-arches and new side sills designed to cover some extra-wide wheel-and-tyre options that were, of course, drawn from the Wolfrace catalogue.

The Wolf Design Sport pictured here was primarily intended to display the new wheels from British specialists Wolfrace, but an eye-catching wide-arch bodykit also helped.

As the rear number-plate reveals, the bodykit on the Wolf Design Sport came from Ibher Design, a Portuguese company.

CHAPTER TEN

BUYING AND OWNING AN L320 SPORT

One day it may be quite difficult to find an L320 Range Rover Sport in good original condition. A quite high proportion of examples (in Britain, at least) have been passed down through the second-hand market to owners who are more inclined to spend money on big wheels and a loud exhaust than they are on regular servicing, and the Sport does not take kindly to neglect. It is a complex vehicle with quite enough to go wrong from regular wear and tear, without the assistance of skimped maintenance – and when major problems do arise, they are likely to be beyond the budget of the typical third, fourth or fifth owner. At the time of writing, for example, removing the body from the chassis (necessary for some engine work) was likely to cost around £1,500 before the work itself could actually be done.

Figures like that present a serious deterrent, with the result that many owners have been tempted to bodge a repair or to move the vehicle on to a new and unsuspecting owner as quickly as possible.

For that reason, a top priority when buying a used Sport is a thick file of servicing receipts. The basic requirement for all models of Sport is a service every 24,000km (15,000 miles) or twelve months, and the diesel engines need a cambelt change every 170,000km (105,000 miles) or seven years. The service schedule also calls for a full coolant change every ten years, and a full change of brake fluid every three years. Major services are needed every six years (for the TDV8) or every seven years (6-cylinder diesels and petrol V8s), and these will be expensive.

The Sport makes a fine family vehicle. This picture shows a TDV6 demonstrator from Land Rover's press fleet, which the author borrowed for a family holiday in France.

The L320 Sport did not attract many orders from the emergency services in Britain, probably on the grounds of cost, but Land Rover did try with this 2010-model police demonstrator.

RELIABILITY

It is very quick and easy these days to get an idea of what almost any reasonably modern car is like to own by looking for interest groups on social media. That is very much the case with the L320 Sport, which has attracted a very enthusiastic group of owners who are more than happy to talk about their vehicles. However, it is worth sounding a note of caution here. As with other makes of car that have attracted such a 'fan base', it is very often the people who have had bad experiences who contribute the largest number of postings; the ones who have nothing to complain about rarely contribute anything like as much.

As a result, it is very easy to get the impression that ownership of a Sport is a constant and expensive headache. It can be – but if you do your best to look after it, maintain it to the standards recommended by Land Rover, and don't depart too far from the standard specification, ownership can be both enjoyable and rewarding. It would be misleading to describe the L320 as inherently unreliable, but it would be accurate to say that there are some things that can go wrong with it that can be very expensive to put right. It might also be accurate to say that the major things usually go wrong when an owner has failed to keep maintenance up to the mark or has made some modifications.

Not surprisingly, the newer models give less trouble than the older ones, although it is debatable whether that is the result of genuine improvements in build quality, or of the greater length of time the older ones have had to be neglected. It's also worth noting that owners generally report more trouble with the convenience gadgets (most of which are electronic) than with the structure or the mechanical hardware of the Sport. In simple terms, that means that there is less to go wrong in a model with a lower specification.

THE HANDBOOK

Land Rover provided a comprehensive owner's handbook with every Sport it made, and that handbook is an essential document for getting to understand your vehicle properly. It is, admittedly, not very exciting to read, but on a vehicle with this sort of complexity it is a first port of call when trying to work out how to operate some systems (especially those operated by a touch screen) or when trying to find where a particular fuse or relay is located in order to check that it is functioning correctly.

Note that Land Rover were well aware of the complexity of the Sport, and that the handbook was necessarily similarly complex. So they provided every new vehicle with a smaller 'Quick Start Guide' to enable an owner to get to grips with the vehicle quickly. This handbook is a bare minimum for anyone who buys a Sport today.

Do not buy a Range Rover Sport without at least one of these handbooks – or, if the vehicle is so good that its condition over-rides this advice, then make sure to find a handbook as quickly as you can through eBay or perhaps at an autojumble. Make sure that the handbook is the right one for your vehicle, because there were so many changes of specification over the years that the handbook for, say, a 2006 model will be of limited use for a 2011 car.

COSTS

The L320 Sport was not designed to be run by owners with a very small budget, and it does not take kindly to such use. It will usually treat you as well as you treat it – and that means spending money as and when it is needed. Although a routine service once a year might cost no more than £400 (at the time of writing) from a non-franchised specialist garage, you should always be prepared for extra costs that come from the need for replacement belts, filters and the like.

Tyres, too, are not cheap. For that reason, it's advisable to keep the suspension in good order and to make sure that any signs of uneven wear are investigated right away. The Sport may be an off-roader, but its tyres are still vulnerable to kerbing damage.

There's a limited amount you can do to reduce the high running costs. You can use the vehicle less (which will increasingly become the case as surviving examples get treated as pampered classics), or you can choose one of the more frugal engines. However, in Britain at least, road tax and insurance will always be on the expensive side.

Power, prestige – and high costs!

WHAT IS IT GOOD AT?

There are all kinds of reasons for owning, or wanting to own, a Range Rover Sport. In some cases, the key reason is the model's carefully honed image as the fashionable transport of celebrities – but bear in mind that tarted-up, worn-out examples also have an image of being associated with drug dealers.

Most importantly, though, there is the feel-good factor that comes from driving one. This is a Range Rover, after all, and the command driving position is unsurpassed in the automotive world. You sit high up where you can see over the traffic ahead; you have excellent all-round visibility; and the passenger cabin itself exudes an aura of luxury, especially in models where wood and leather are combined.

On the road, the Sport is very enjoyable to drive. It was deliberately designed with sharp handling and performance, which, back in 2005, were uncommon in a large SUV, and although it cannot be flung about like a small hatchback, it is both sporty and sure-footed. Off the road, all that needs to be said is that this is a Land Rover at heart, and it will do what that name suggests.

For some people, a key element in the Sport's appeal is its towing ability. With a maximum towing weight of 3,500kg (7,700lb) – or 750kg (1,655lb) if the trailer is unbraked – these vehicles make light work of even the largest caravans, and will also comfortably tow gliders, speedboats, or other cars on trailers.

The Sport made a superb towing vehicle in the well-established Land Rover tradition. This press picture was issued to mark its selection as AXA Lesiure Car of the Year 2006–2007 by the Ulster Group of Motoring Writers.

WHICH TO BUY?

As already mentioned, it is vitally important to buy an L320 Sport that has been properly cared for, so make your choice carefully: a bad example will become a money-pit. Condition must always be the number one factor in influencing your decision to purchase.

Your choice of an L320 will otherwise probably be governed primarily by its engine, and there are some thoughts on this below. High levels of equipment may also sway the

Always assess a potential purchase very carefully. This example was pictured passing through an auction house in Australia in 2013.

This early 2010 model was placed with the West Midlands Fire Service, who used it as an incident commander's vehicle.

issue, but in many cases are really not worth holding out for, because all Sports were well equipped, even the entry-level S models that were available before mid-2009. Again, see below for some further thoughts on this.

WHICH ENGINE?

Realistically, most Range Rover Sports you will find for sale in Europe are likely to have one of the TDV6 diesel engines. In the USA and some other countries, of course, only the petrol models were ever available.

The TDV6 diesels undoubtedly offer the best fuel economy, and 9.4ltr/100km (30mpg) or more is possible on long steady runs. However, there is a world of difference between the 2.7-litre single-turbo engine and the later (2010 model-year on) 3.0-litre twin-turbo engine. The 2.7-litre is adequate and gives good, solid performance, but it is no ball of fire, and press-on drivers are likely to find it a little frustrating at times. It can feel slow when accelerating away from rest, and it is not uncommon to find that an owner has had a TDV6 engine 'chipped' to improve that acceleration.

The 3.0-litre engine simply transformed the experience of driving a diesel Sport, delivering quite exhilarating accel-

eration (for a vehicle of this type) without the penalty of an increase in fuel consumption. The SDV6 version of this engine (on 2012 and later models) brought even more top-end power and an eight-speed automatic gearbox, which made its own contribution to good fuel economy. In fact, a gently driven SDV6 model can return up to about 8.8ltr/100km (32mpg), although enjoying its performance too much will certainly do some damage to its fuel consumption. The emissions of the SDV6 engine were also lower than those of the earlier 3.0-litre TDV6 (they dropped from 243g/km to 230g/km), which may result in some annual taxation savings in some countries.

Many commentators argue that the best engine of them all is the TDV8, and it is hard to argue with that point of view. The engine has simply enormous torque (more than that of the contemporary supercharged petrol V8), which gives smooth, refined, and very rapid acceleration. It is a very free-revving engine, but it is not as frugal as the 6-cylinder diesels, and around 11ltr/100km (25mpg) is probably about average as a consumption figure. However, the TDV8 is much less common than either of the TDV6 engines, and because of its strong reputation there is likely to be a rush of buyers when one comes up for sale. That in turn will ensure that the seller keeps the price high.

The V8 engines deliver a superb drive – this is an early 4.4-litre type – but most owners in Europe settle for one of the diesels.

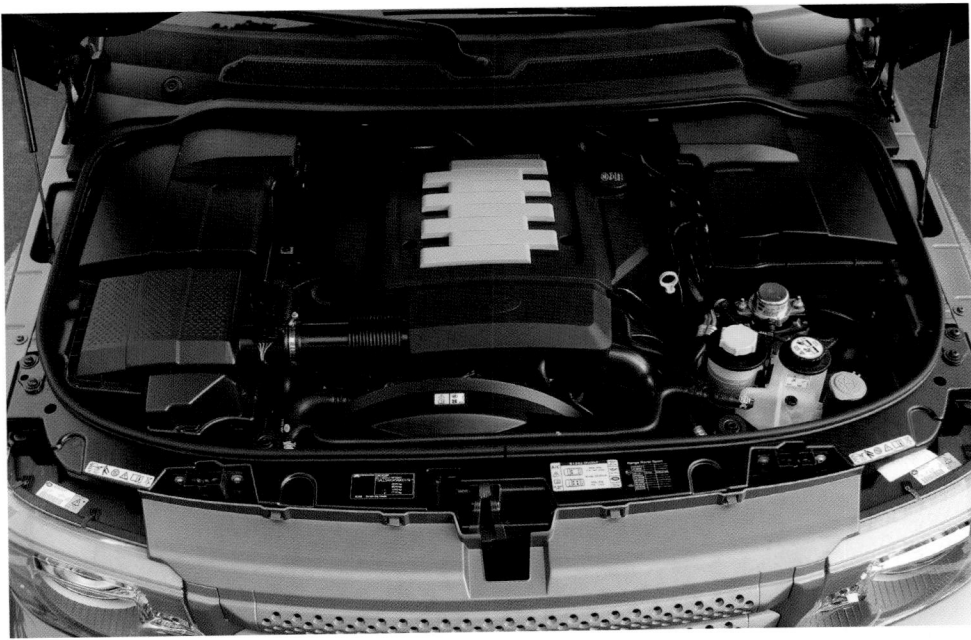

There is not much to see under the bonnet of any Sport, except a large plastic cosmetic engine cover. At least this one reveals that it is the supercharged V8 – in this case an early 4.2-litre type.

As for the naturally aspirated V8 petrol engines, only the 4.4-litre type was sold in Europe, and that was withdrawn in 2007; the 5.0-litre naturally aspirated type was never made available, although it became the core engine in North America and in some other countries. Either will return about 14ltr/100km (20mpg) at best. Both the 4.2-litre and 5.0-litre supercharged engines were sold in Europe, but they are much less common than the diesels. Either one of them will probably return around 16.6–15.7ltr/100km (17–18mpg) on a regular basis, but consumption soars if you indulge in their acceleration too often – and their performance is exhilarating enough that you are very likely to do so!

Old and new: a very late L320 Sport was pictured next to one of the first Range Rover Evoque models in the showrooms of Alfardan Premier Motors in Qatar.

BODYWORK

The large flat doors of the Sport are unforgiving about revealing minor dents, but the good news is that bodywork corrosion in general is rare unless there has been accident damage that has been poorly repaired. Rust may appear on the trim between the body and the window glass, but is usually dealt with fairly easily. The L320's body is predominantly made of steel, and in this respect it differs from many other Land Rover products. The good news associated with this is that repairs are simpler and cheaper than on aluminium body panels.

It is not uncommon to find that door handles cease to work, and the cause of this is usually failure of one of the central locking motors, leaving the lock jammed in the closed position. The sensors for the park distance control system can also give trouble, either giving false warnings (especially in wet weather) or failing to work altogether. It's as well to make sure these are clean whenever you wash the vehicle – and to keep an eye open for their frames losing paint and starting to rust.

If you suspect that a vehicle offered for sale may have been in an accident, take a good look at the door and bonnet hinges, where cracked or missing paint may indicate that the panel was displaced in a collision. At the rear, the cradle for the spare wheel below the load area can get damaged if the vehicle has been reversed over a low bollard or similar obstacle.

A ready means of distinguishing early from late models is by the position of the Range Rover name on the tailgate. On early ones, it is on a grey plinth at the bottom edge; on 2010 and 2011 models, that plinth is body coloured; and on 2012 and 2013 models with the powered tailgate, the name moves up to a position just below the rear window.

TRIM AND EQUIPMENT

The only variants of the L320 Sport that had fabric upholstery were the entry-level S-specification models available before summer 2009. All the others have leather upholstery, and, as the earlier chapters in this book explain, there are several different types of that. One way or another, the passenger cabin always feels well equipped and luxurious, even on those entry-level models. Air conditioning and electric windows are, of course, standard on all variants of the Sport.

It is worth remembering that the lighter interior colours show wear and dirt more readily than the darker ones, and that although the upholstery generally wears very well, the outer bolster on the driver's seat cushion will be the first area to show serious wear. There's a good chance that the rear seats have hardly been used unless the Sport you are looking at has done time as family transport. Some people complain that the rear seats are a little hard for long journeys, but you will need to make up your own mind about that.

There was a wide choice of extra-cost options when these models were new, and many buyers took advantage of the fact. As a result, relatively few examples were supplied with a standard specification; buyers typically set a budget (or their employers set a budget if it was to be a company car) and added as many extras as they could afford. Some extras were, frankly, trivial, but the higher-specification sound systems, heated windscreen and heated seats are among those that are genuinely worth having.

Most of the desirable and commonly specified extras were plumbed into the car's electrical system, about which more in a moment. The more of this equipment there is, the more carefully you will need to check that it works when looking over an L320 Sport that is for sale. Some problems are minor – heated seat failures and central locking problems do not cost a lot to repair – but others can be quite expensive. That's why many owners don't bother to fix them when they show up.

It is worth singling out the satellite navigation system that is built into many examples of the Sport. The early type was a little clunky in operation and will seem outdated to anyone used to a more modern system. Updates were available from time to time, and the very newest roads and housing developments will not show up on a system where these have not been installed. Check the availability of updates with your Land Rover dealer (and expect them to be quite expensive if they can still be had).

MECHANICAL PROBLEMS

Problems don't only arise on other people's cars, and should make you wary when you're looking at one that's for sale. Those same problems may eventually affect a Sport that you own yourself, so it's worth having a good idea of what can go wrong in order to take appropriate action when necessary. What follows is by no means an exhaustive list, but it should give you some idea of the major mechanical problems that affect the Sport.

Some Sports suffer with vibration through the steering wheel, which is transmitted from the steering rack. Land Rover developed a cure for this, which involved fitting a special damper, and it is worth asking whether this has been fitted to a car that is for sale. Other vibrations may be due to uneven tyre wear, in which case the cause needs to be investigated.

Brakes are powerful servo-assisted discs with ABS as standard, and should stop the vehicle very quickly in an emergency. Listen out for the standard brake problems, such as squeal (sometimes resulting from badly worn pads meeting discs when the brakes are applied), and get any vibration or uneven pulling to one side looked at as soon as possible.

Never a dull moment: this Sport was dressed up as an advertisement for a local beer when it took part in the Coamo Expedition in Puerto Rico during July 2007.
CARIBBEAN ROVERS

Owners are understandably often tempted to buy aftermarket (cheaper) brake components when items need to be changed, but this is often a false economy. Some aftermarket pads wear very quickly, and in all cases brake-pad life may be limited because the Sport is a heavy vehicle to stop. A lot will depend on how you drive it.

Above all, never be tempted to buy cheap replacement parts for one of the Supercharged models. The special Brembo brake callipers were used for a very good reason, and they deserve high-quality pads at replacement time.

Step-off from rest should be smooth and quite spritely with all the different engines, but if a TDV6 seems to hesitate when pulling away, the cause is probably a choked EGR (exhaust gas recirculation) valve, which needs to be replaced every 65,000km (40,000 miles). In some countries this valve is a legal requirement and must be replaced, but in others it can be blanked off; an inexpensive kit is available to do the job.

Poor acceleration and performance in general from a 2.7-litre TDV6 might indicate that the turbocharger is on the way out. If so, be prepared for a major bill, because the accepted fix requires the body to be removed from the chassis first. Some specialists have found ways round this that bring the cost down, but you should ask exactly what they do, and ensure that you are happy with it before committing to such a repair.

All Sports had an automatic gearbox, which is a six-speed type on all except the late SDV6 models. Some people find the six-speed gearbox a little slow to respond. Both the six-speed and eight-speed types are generally robust and reliable, but early six-speed types had a problem with the parking pawl failing to engage properly. Further back along the drivetrain, the input bearing on the transfer gearbox can wear and become noisy. The bearing itself is cheap enough, but replacement involves taking the transfer box out – and that is quite a major job.

AIR SUSPENSION

There is no reason to be frightened of the air suspension that is standard on all Sports. It is a robust and reliable system, although of course it has its weaknesses, too.

The air springs (people often call them 'air bags', which can be confusing) must be treated as consumable items. They are essentially hollow rubber cylinders, and over time their constant flexing and chafing will cause them to leak. Air springs should last for 65,000km (40,000 miles) or so, but problems should always be attended to as soon as they occur. A leaking air spring will cause the compressor to work extra hard in an attempt to keep it inflated, and eventually the compressor will burn out. Compressors are expensive. If a Sport sits low over one wheel, the air spring is clearly not holding pressure and will have to be replaced. It is obviously not a good idea to drive far with the suspension down on its bump stops because of failed springs or a failed compressor.

Height sensors can also fail, so they do not send a signal to the compressor that requests air to be pumped into the associated spring. There is no known way of predicting that this failure is about to happen, but the evidence that something is wrong will be only too clear when the vehicle sits down over one wheel. Sometimes it is possible to guess that this is the problem if the compressor cannot be heard running and the vehicle body will not rise to the correct ride height.

The weight of the Sport also means that suspension bushes will wear over time, and that wear is likely to be accelerated if oversize wheels have been fitted. Clunks and creaks from the suspension are a good indication that bushes may need attention.

WHEELS AND TYRES

All Sports ran on alloy wheels, and Land Rover supplied a wide variety of styles in sizes up to and including a 20in diameter. Some people like the wheel rims to be as large as possible because of their appearance, but unfortunately the larger-diameter wheels have to be fitted with tyres that have shallower sidewalls. These are not only detrimental to the ride quality but often allow the alloy wheel rims to make rough contact with kerbs and the like, so causing damage.

If you have (or are planning to buy) a Sport with 17in, 18in or 19in wheels and are thinking about changing to a larger diameter wheel, remember that Land Rover specified a damped steering rack with 20in wheels to maintain the original steering and suspension geometry.

If you are intending to do any serious off-road driving with a Sport, it is always better to use a wheel size that allows the deepest possible tyre sidewalls. Low-profile tyres are more readily damaged in off-road use and are not recommended for it.

ELECTRICAL SYSTEM

The heart of a Sport's electrical system is its battery, and it is vitally important to keep this up to the mark. Never fit a lower-capacity battery than the one recommended just because it is cheaper. The electrical system depends on a reliable 12-volt supply, and if the current available drops too low, the system will typically trigger a variety of warning lights and dashboard messages. A failing alternator will lead to the same rash of problems.

Beware of the engine management system warning light on the dashboard, which needs investigation at once if it will not go out after the standard automatic system check on start-up. It may be triggered by such things as a failed water pump (particularly on the petrol engines), but it may also point to wider electrical problems.

Other electrical problems are often self-evident, but quite common ones include missing pixels on the dashboard message centre and – very annoying, this – a fuel pump that fails without warning.

OFF THE ROAD

Relatively few owners of a Range Rover Sport use it for anything more difficult than driving on loose gravel or driving across a muddy field. That is a pity, because the L320 was designed with all the traditional off-road ability of a Land Rover, plus some more besides.

The Sport was one of the first Land Rover models to feature Terrain Response, which sets a number of systems to deliver the most appropriate behaviour for the type of terrain over which the vehicle is being driven. This removes a great deal of the responsibility for 'getting it right' from the driver – although of course it cannot overcome the laws of physics. All Sports also came with Hill Descent Control, which limits speed downhill in low range to prevent the vehicle running away out of control. Then there is the height-adjustable air suspension, which can lift the body to allow it to clear a tricky obstacle.

The L320 Sport has an approach angle of 30–34 degrees depending on the suspension height setting, a departure angle of 26–29 degrees, and a break-over angle of 20–25 degrees. This is not the place to go into further detail about these measurements, but it is enough to say that they prevent the underside from grounding in most rough terrain. It also has a maximum wading depth of 700mm (27in) in standard form, which means that it will wade through water that is as deep as the tops of the wheels.

The Sport's off-road capability often amazes owners, and it is only too common to hear them say that their nerve

The Sport is a Land Rover in the true tradition, and is formidably capable off-road as well as on it. This one is pictured doing some rock crawling in the USA.

gave out before the vehicle showed any signs of faltering. It is, without any doubt, a proper Land Rover.

AFTERMARKET MODIFICATIONS

If a Sport you are examining with a view to purchase has been modified with aftermarket accessories, it is important to identify exactly what these are. They typically include styling kits, engine and suspension changes, and non-original (usually bigger) wheels. First, you want to know what these items are, to make sure that they do not compromise the safety or reliability of the vehicle. Second, you need to know where they came from, because if they become damaged, it will be no use going to your local Land Rover dealership for replacements.

RECALLS

Most modern cars get 'recalled' by their makers when some unsuspected problem crops up, and dealers then attend to that problem with an authorized fix free of charge. This happened to the L320 Sport five times during its production life, which is actually quite a good record for a car of such complexity. All the problems identified should have been rectified under warranty, but it is worth knowing what they were, and (when buying a car) perhaps asking to see proof in the service records that the recall action was carried out.

In **November 2005**, very early Sports were recalled to deal with the risk of a seatbelt buckle not locking correctly; and secondly, to rectify a fault with the park function in the automatic gearbox.

In **June 2006**, the recall looked at balance weights fitted on the insides of the wheels that could foul sensors and brake hoses.

In **September 2009**, there were two recalls: one checked for oil getting into the brake booster and reducing braking efficiency; the other checked for a leak from the fuel pump.

PRODUCTION FIGURES

The following tables record the serial number of the first L320 produced in each month. For a guide to the serial number sequences, see Appendix II.

	2003	2004	2005	2006	2007	2008
Jan			900227	939921	998347	160215
Feb			900499	945333	104067	166483
Mar			901468	950701	109373	172365
Apr		000573	903079	956781	115372	176349
May			905843	960669	120075	181550
June			909232	965977	124751	185233
July	000500	900000	913229	971638	130170	189781
Aug	000503	900002	916352	975573	133988	193739
Sep	000512	900018	919347	980026	138773	196339
Oct	000529	900046	924914	985497	144408	200748
Nov	000548	900071	929263	989744	149360	203173
Dec	000556	900121	935377	995434	155711	204857
TOTAL	72	231	39,694	58,426	61,868	45,755

	2009	2010	2011	2012	2013
Jan	205970	235167	282519	737980	795857
Feb	207026	238967	286981	742657	801583
Mar	209204	242860	292047	747473	807681
Apr	211177	247359	297875	752899	
May	212541	251148	702223	756871	
June	213400	254669	706843	762465	
July	215623	258283	711731	766831	
Aug	217364	262012	715873	772935	
Sep	219848	264792	718633	777032	
Oct	224087	269637	724436	783269	
Nov	227403	272989	727787	787598	
Dec	231762	278288	733243	792377	
TOTAL	29,197	47,445	58,459	57,878	14,816

Grand Total: 413,841

VIN IDENTIFICATION AND DATING

The VIN of an L320 Sport will be found on a sticker attached to the front panel underneath the bonnet, and is repeated on a tag visible through the base of the windscreen on the passenger's side.

The format of an RoW (Rest of the World, i.e. not NAS) VIN is an eleven-character alphanumeric type identifier, followed by a six-figure serial number. The NAS (North American Specification) VINs also have an eleven-digit prefix code followed by a six-figure serial number, but the interpretation of the prefix codes differs.

ROW VINS

A theoretical RoW VIN might be SALLSAA135A-123456. This breaks down as shown in the table below (alternatives for each position are also shown).

SAL	Land Rover
LS	L320
A	Standard trim
	J = Japan
A	Four doors
I	2.7-litre TDV6 engine
	2 = 3.6-litre V8
	3 = 4.2-litre supercharged V8
	5 = 4.4-litre V8
	7 = 3.6-litre TDV8 with DPF
	D = 5.0-litre V8
	E = 5.0-litre supercharged V8
	F = 3.0-litre TDV6 or SDV6
	G = 3.0-litre TDV6 or SDV6 with DPF
	? = 4.4-litre TDV8
3	RHD with automatic gearbox
	4 = LHD with automatic gearbox
5	2005MY
	6 = 2006
	7 = 2007
	8 = 2008
	9 = 2009
	A = 2010
	B = 2011
	C = 2012
	D = 2013
A	Solihull (assembly plant)
123456	Serial number

NAS VINS

A theoretical NAS VIN might be SALLSAA135A-123456. This breaks down as shown in the table below (alternatives for each position are also shown).

SAL	Land Rover
S	L320
A	Standard trim
	B = S trim
	D = SE trim
	F = HSE trim
	H = Supercharged
2	Four doors
3	4.2-litre supercharged V8 engine
	5 = 4.4-litre V8
	D = 5.0-litre V8
	E = 5.0-litre supercharged V8
4	LHD with automatic gearbox
0	Check digit (0 to 9, or X)
5	2005MY
	6 = 2006
	7 = 2007
	8 = 2008
	9 = 2009
	A = 2010
	B = 2011
	C = 2012
	D = 2013
A	Solihull (assembly plant)
123456	Serial number

SERIAL NUMBER SEQUENCES

The same serial number sequences were used for both RoW and NAS vehicles.

000500 to 000576	Prototype models, 2003–2004
900000 to 99999	2004–2007
100000 to 199999	2007–2008
200000 to 29999	2008–2011
700000 to 79999	2011–2013
800000 to 808500 approx.	2013

RANGE ROVER SPORT PRICES IN THE UK

These figures are showroom prices for Range Rover Sport models without extras. All figures are on-the-road (OTR) and inclusive of Value Added Tax (VAT).

Date	Model	Price
2005, June	TDV6 S	£35,000
	TDV6 SE	£40,000
	TDV6 HSE	£44,000
	V8 S	£45,000
	V8 HSE	£50,000
	Supercharged	£57,500
	First Edition Supercharged	£59,000
2006, January	TDV6 S	£35,500
	TDV6 SE	£40,500
	TDV6 HSE	£44,500
	V8 SE	£45,500
	V8 HSE	£50,500
	V8 Supercharged	£58,000
2006, June	Supercharged HST	£63,000
2006, November	TDV6 S	£35,665
	TDV6 SE	£40,665
	TDV6 HSE	£47,265
	TDV8 HSE	£53,120
	TDV8 HST	£59,020
	V8 HSE	£54,500
	Supercharged HSE	£57,325
	Supercharged HST	£63,225
2007, May	TDV6 S	£35,750
	TDV6 SE	£42,450
	TDV6 HSE	£47,700
	TDV8 HSE	£53,550
	V8 Supercharged	£57,750
2007, December	TDV6 S	£35,750
	TDV6 SE	£42,450

Date	Model	Price
	TDV6 HSE	£47,700
	TDV8 HSE	£54,250
	Supercharged HSE	£57,750
2008, March	TDV6 XS	£39,995
	TDV8 HST	£59,995
2008, July	TDV6 S	£38,495
	TDV6 SE	£43,095
	TDV6 HSE	£48,495
	TDV8 HSE	£55,095
	TDV8 HST	£60,795
	Supercharged HSE	£59,595
	Supercharged HST	£63,895
2009, March	TDV6 Stormer edition	£43,550
2009, September	TDV6 SE	£44,895
	TDV6 HSE	£50,695
	TDV8 HSE	£56,995
	Supercharged HSE	£61,995
2010, January	TDV8 Sport Autobiography	£65,145
	V8 Supercharged Autobiography Sport	£69,995
2011, November	HSE 3.0 SDV6	£55,995
2012, June	HSE Red SDV6	£58,020
	HSE Luxury SDV6	£58,020
2013, April	SDV6 SE	£50,220
	SDV6 HSE Black Edition	£57,920
	SDV6 Autobiography Sport	£68,020
	V8 Supercharged Autobiography Sport	£76,330

INDEX